Through the Eye of A Needle: Keys from An Ancient Pre-Historic Teaching Across Time and Space

Fourth Edition

Gilbert Moore

A Blue Logic Publication
http://bluelogic.us/
All rights reserved © 2022
Copyright throughout the world

ISBN 978-1-08792-738-1

"Enter, therefore and pass in through the secret gates, and you shall go in and come out as you desire."

An Egyptian holy book

Book 1: Through the Eye of A Needle

2009

CONTENTS

I have learned so much from God
That I can no longer call myself
A Christian, a Hindu, a Muslim,
a Buddhist, a Jew.

The Truth has shared so much of Itself
With me that I can no longer call
Myself a man, a woman, an angel,
Or even a pure soul.

Love has befriended Hafiz
so completely It has turned to ash
And freed me of every concept
And image my mind has ever known.

                              Hafiz, The Gift

AUTHOR'S NOTE: THE DREAM

I

Twilight: Dark clouds rolling in, lightning flashes. Cracks in barren earth begin to open up in front of us, behind us, to the left and to the right as far as one can see to the horizon. Those of us on one side of the fault lines somehow know we are safe, the Teacher is next to us. We reach out to our loved ones on the other side – to other students of the Teacher, to relatives, friends -- to join us. They refuse, and we watch helplessly as the earth opens and they begin receding farther and farther and faster and faster away from us.

This dream occurred on the night of June 6, 2006.

Gilbert Moore

I. Taking things too literally -- even dreams

The Path of Masters derives its substance in unbroken succession from the earliest times. It maintains its connection, in a parallel way, with both the ancients and the contemporary teachers by direct communication of being.

Baudddin Naqshband

In Italy, on the floor of the Cathedral of Siena, there is a mosaic showing a tall bearded elderly man in a broad-brimmed hat wearing fine robes and standing in front of a man and woman, both middle-aged. His left hand rests on a square-shaped stone tablet with an inscription carved in Latin. The tablet sits on a pair of stone winged lions. Between the two lions there is a herald staff of two serpents intertwined in the shape of a figure eight.

The elderly man is smiling compassionately at the man and woman, perhaps decoding the Latin for them or perhaps simply looking into their eyes and being present to them, and they to him, no words. Written below this scene is an inscription: "Hermes Mercurius Trismegistus Siena Cathedral." [1]

Literally, that's all there is: An elderly man with a compassionate smile, perhaps explaining to a man and a woman the meaning of some obscure teaching carved in stone in Latin or perhaps simply being the message itself without words. Beware: There is much more in this floor mosaic, much, much more.

Hidden in the imagery of fine robes, winged lions and intertwined serpents, there is an inner meaning. Existing for thousands of years, a tradition of metaphor and allegory called the *hermetic tradition* has been teaching those of us with eyes, ears and an open heart how to retrieve this meaning and transmit it to others. We call it *hermeneutics*, not knowing what we're really talking about.

The studies in this volume represent an attempt to continue this tradition.

The evolution and descent of outer meanings. Seen from one point of view, human languages serve primarily a sensory-motor, instinctive-emotional and intellectual function, and always have. To feel, visualize, think about and communicate vocally whatever one wants or needs out there (around ones lower self) or in here (usually inside ones head or stomach) in this moment or doesn't want is the only real issue. The meaning of life reduces to having food, drink, warmth, sex, conviviality, wealth, and power, nothing more. *There is no hidden, inner meaning, no enigma, no riddle.*

From this point of view, as civilizations advance and decline and advance again, the evolution of language is simply a record of the increasing complexity of communicating simple needs and desires. The original impulse to feel, visualize, etc. honestly is still there, but covered up and lost more often than not beneath layer after layer of fabrication: buffers, unintended lies, and distortions. Languages are also an integral part of humanity's tool-making/tool-using impulse, an inventive impulse which shows up in mathematics, reaches increasing levels of complexity in science and engineering, and feeds back continuously into more technical innovations. To mix metaphors, human language is a Tower of Babel, a Satanic machine in perpetual motion leading to the invention of electricity, the Internet and stem cell research, but also to hydrogen warheads and biochemical weapons.

Ladders of self-remembering. There is, however, another point of view. Without rejecting literal-minded claims, this other view adds another significant dimension: revelation – mystical, poetic, mathematical, scientific, with or without hallucinogenics.. In Lewis Carroll's *Alice in Wonderland* there is a remarkable exchange between Alice and Humpty Dumpty shortly before his fatal fall:

'As I was saying' Humpty Dumpty said, 'That SEEMS to be done right--though I haven't time to look it over thoroughly just now--and that shows that there are three hundred and sixty-four days when you might get un-birthday presents--'

'Certainly,' said Alice.

'And only ONE for birthday presents, you know. There's glory for you!'

'I don't know what you mean by "glory,"' Alice said.

Humpty Dumpty smiled contemptuously. 'Of course you don't-- till I tell you. I meant "there's a nice knock-down argument for you!"'

'But "glory" doesn't mean "a nice knock-down argument,"' Alice objected.

'When I use a word,' Humpty Dumpty said in rather a scornful tone, 'it means just what I choose it to mean--neither more nor less.'

'The question is,' said Alice, 'whether you CAN make words mean so many different things.'

'The question is,' said Humpty Dumpty, 'which is to be master-- that's all.'

Once the dimension of revelation is added, fissures and cracks begin to open up in the functionally defined universe of literal mindedness. Words lose their anchor in things and begin drifting from meaning one thing to meaning something else. "Glory", for example, comes to mean "many different things", including "a nice knockdown argument." Even worse, there is no guarantee that a thing is or will remain as it first appears. In the universe of God communicating to humanity and humanity to God literal-mindedness becomes a liability. Why is that?

Premises of the literal-minded. Taking things literally has always been a necessary evil: A robber holds you at gunpoint demanding money or your life. This is no occasion for interpreting his demand allegorically. On an architectural blueprint the dimensions of a door reads 4 feet wide by 8 feet high, the building contractor reads these dimensions literally, not metaphorically, sawing and nailing into place a 4 foot by 8 foot door. A high jump bar has been set at 6 feet 10 inches, the athlete will jump just a little higher than that clearing the bar, or he won't. There is no hidden message in his success or failure.

The question is: must everything be taken literally? When is it appropriate to do so, and when is it not? The consensus is that it is best not to take literally the *Bible,* Homer's *Iliad,* Plato's *Dialogues* or Shakespeare's *Love Sonnets* or his *Tempest, Midsummer Nights Dream and Winter's Tale.* One can take their imagery and stories literally, but to do so is to strip away and impoverish them of so very much meaning, one is left with linguistic skeletons (and at worst booby traps), it means reducing those works to the level of reality represented by sawing and nailing a wooden door into place.

Where and how is one to draw the line between literal-mindedness and metaphor. Time and continual loss of memory are not making matters any easier -- a fact compounded by the tendency of humanity's inner circle to conceal the keys to understanding its own works and those of others. "The Pharisees and the Scribes have received the keys of Knowledge", Jesus is reported to have said, "They have hidden[the keys]. They did not wished." (Gospel of Thomas 88:39) In their obsession with hiding the divine light from others some within the inner circle inevitably hide it from themselves.

The main premise for literal-mindedness is its chief fallacy: Whatever is stated or written, including statements about God and miracles, need only be understood functionally to exhaust its meaning, that is, it needs only be understood in terms of what can be seen, felt, heard or thought – at least in principle. Metaphor, analogy and allegory are poorly understood, if understood at all. Literal-mindedness represents the thinking of the mechanical parts of our machines, that is, the intellectual, emotional instinctive moving parts operating on automatic pilot.

This premise leads to some curious results: Humanity can be traced back literally to an Original Couple living in the Garden of Eden (by the way, moving in literally around 9:00 AM on September 12, 4,700 BC). The First Woman Eve is seduced there by a talkative scheming serpent into eating the forbidden fruit. Fast-forward: Besides Noah and his family, a Great Flood literally destroys humanity,

Moses literally looks to the right and sees a burning bush and hears God talking out of it; the Virgin Birth is literally just that: Mary conceiving Jesus without being impregnated by Joseph. And finally: Judas literally betrays Jesus for 30 shekals of silver, and the rotting corpse of Jesus literally rises from the dead after three days and travels with his disciples before ascending to heaven.

If one is not to understand these stories literally, how then is one to understand them?

Metaphor and allegory. For tens of thousands of years humanity has been using a variety of oral and written forms of communication to encrypt and decode the inner meaning of higher state revelations – sacred images, sacred numbers, metaphors, and allegories being the most frequent. And within each one of these encrypted forms there has been a fifth form, wordless and imageless, running parallel to the others and producing presence. This fifth form has gone by many names – "the divine manifesting itself in man", the "Tao", the "Subtle Origin", the "Seed of Osiris". Here we call it simply *conscious shocks producing presence.*[3]

Communication by metaphor and allegory has been the common denominator of every major esoteric school beginning with the cave painting shamans of prehistoric South Africa and Europe and extending through the Ancient Egyptian priesthoods at Memphis and Luxor across time to the Platonists, Philokalia Desert Fathers, Sufi's, Cabbalists and Fourth Way of modern times.

The Fourth Way tradition is the youngest, being less than 100 years old as of this writing (2008 AD) and the encrypting methods found in pre-historic cave paintings are the oldest (the earliest being about 100,000 years old). Unifying these traditions across thousands of years and vast cultural differences is *the principle (and miracle) of invariance,* the Hermetic Rosetta Stone: Each encrypting and decoding tradition is interchangeable with the others and ultimately yields the same inner meaning as these others.

Encrypting and decoding hieroglyphs. While it is not the oldest tradition, the ancient Egyptian tradition is certainly the most well-preserved, and for this reason it is a useful starting-point for understanding the basic principles of hermetic encryption. The method it shares with other traditions is that of moving from the outer literal meaning to the inner. Interestingly enough, in Ancient Egyptian hieroglyphs this movement from the literal to the esoteric is embedded in the very process of writing and decoding hieroglyphic text.

Encrypting hieroglyphs begins with the inner meaning.; a revelation, a flash of light from higher centers. What is the point of this communication, what purpose is being served? These are first questions, say, in the mind of an anonymous Egyptian priest.[4] Creating a context, a storyline, an allegorical subtext comes next. Finally, the literal meaning: the hieroglyphic images.

Decoding hieroglyphs reverses the process: The first step, *sign-listing* a hieroglyphic image, reveals its outer literal meaning. The second step, *transliterating and then using determinatives* to narrow the context, yields the contextual, metaphorical meaning. The metaphors often appear with a storyline, and this storyline is called an *allegory.* Finally, *keying* the allegory creates the opportunity for conscious shocks. These shocks recover the *inner meaning.* Some examples:

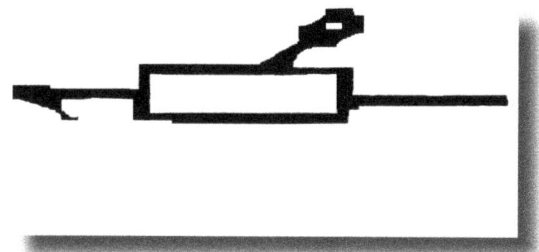

In its simplest form, the hieroglyph for *the number one* is represented by a harpoon. Transliterating this image, we find that its phonetic value is *ua* meaning "one, single or only one." Sometimes this same meaning is communicated with a harpoon and an arm (signifying the indefinite article) and sometimes it is communicated using the image of a chick bird. With a seated bearded man, *Ua* describes one of the gods, "Number One of the Gods" or simply "the One". This became a title for Re, Amun, Osiris, Neith, Sehkmit, Hathor and other divinities. We have passed from the hieroglyph's literal meaning to its contextual meaning—from its outer meanings to the beginning of metaphor and allegory.

The missing third layer of meaning. Keying "One" or "Number One of the Gods" or for that matter Re, Amun, Osiris, etc., as the Ancient Egyptians did and arriving at *the inner meaning they arrived at themselves* does not seem possible for an obvious reason: We do not know how they keyed it, we do not have the *mapping algorithm* they used to encrypt the inner meaning of "one" or "Number One of the Gods". A possible solution to this otherwise insurmountable problem is presented below (in "Fourth Way tradition")

Our second example is the hieroglyph for *the number four.*
The number four is represented by several groups of hieroglyphs. In the one selected for illustrating the inherently
hermetic properties of the Ancient Egyptian the number
four is represented by a reed sign, a horned viper and a
righthand. Transliterating these images produces a contextual meaning with the phonetic value *aft.* Four strokes
at the end of this group serve as the determinative. In this
group it has associations with two and three- dimensional
objects – rectangles and boxes (including the sarcophagus). What did this mean to Ancient Egyptians?

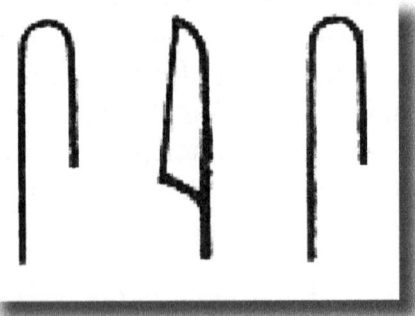

Our next example is the hieroglyph for *the number six.* At

the literal level, the number six is represented in one of two ways: by two folded cloth signs separated by a flowering reed or simply by six strokes. Transliterating both hiero glyphs yields the phonetic value *sas* or simply *su*.

With a sun sign and an alabaster purification bowl as determinatives the six strokes mean "6th day of the festival of purification". When *sas* appears in one of its two forms with the garment sign as the determinative, it means "six-threaded stuff" or "a six-threaded garment".

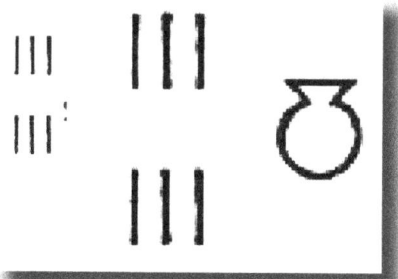

Our final hieroglyph is the hieroglyph for *light:* On the literal level it consists of a reed, an Egyptian hawk and a sieve combining with an image of the sun radiating nine rays of light to form a hieroglyph with the phonetic value *aaku.* Having the same phonetic value, a crested ibis bird often replaces the reed-Egyptian hawk image. The contextual meanings of *aaku* are numerous: light, radiant soul, beautiful deeds, splendid acts, virtues and blessings. What about the inner meaning for Ancient Egyptians?

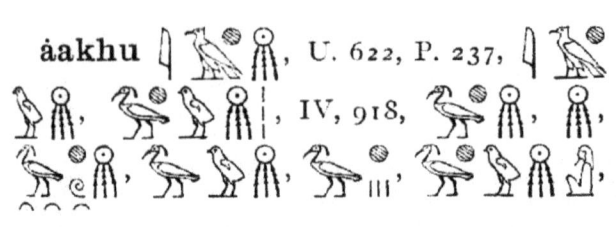

Prehistoric cave paintings. A perverse law of entropy seems to be at work: the farther back in time we go from the present the more hermetic information we lose. Our Fourth Way tradition, as we will demonstrate below, is still rich in imagery, metaphor, contextual meaning and keys. Going back 800 to a 1,000 years, the immensely rich imageries and allegories of the Sufi tradition are paralleled by a steep dropping off in keys, but thanks to such Sufi masters as Ibn al-Arabi the main ones are still there.[5] Likewise with the traditions of the Philokalia and Neo-Platonists: rich in profound psychological truths (the contextual meaning), but not many keys. In this regard, the Cabalist tradition seems to hold its own. (There is a reason for this difference which we will discuss below. See *Cabalist tradition*).

By the time we reach the Ancient Egyptian Mysteries some 4,500 to 6,000 years ago, we are in the presence of a hermetic tradition that has been stripped *for us* of its keys while retaining information on how to pass from the literal meaning of hieroglyphs to the intermediate contextual meaning. Going even further back, some 25,000 to 100,000 years ago, to prehistoric cave paintings we find that even this layer of intelligibility has been stripped away. We seem to lose two essential layers of information: how to place the cave images in their original context and how to decipher their inner meaning once the contextual meaning has been reconstructed.

Chauvet Caves. Sampling cave images from Chauvet can serve to illustrate the problem. Radiocarbon dating methods place the drawing of the images somewhere between 29, 000 BP and 32,000 BP (BP = before the present era). For our discussion we have selected four cave drawings more or less at random: two showing enigmatic patterns of red dots, a third showing four horses above two rhinos fighting while a third is running away, and a fourth showing ten lions in perspective (or one or two in motion).

The first two images clearly have been stripped of their inner meaning and context, and we are reduced to trying to find meaning in six red dots next to three red stripes in one image and ten red dots in the second. What are we looking at?

The scene of four horses and three rhinos in the third cave painting seems to have more contextual meaning as does the scene of ten lions. But again, the third layer of meaning has been lost. Commenting on the ten lions in perspective, one of its French discoverers noted: "Chauvet Cave reveals that big cats played an unsuspected and important role in the local bestiary [of pre-historic man]." This fact prompts him to hazard an interpretation:

> These animals doubtless symbolized danger, strength and power. But Chauvet Cave was a bear cave, a fact which its first prehistoric explorers could not help but notice. The bear was present through its claw marks, its hollows, its prints, its impressive skeletons, perhaps even its odour. Is it possible that they tried to capture the essence of its power and that of animals that were comparable to it through the danger they represented and the domination they exerted over their environment?

But then he pulls back, retreating into the safety (and comfort) of pure skepticism: "All speculations about this problem can only be guesses.'

The Lewis-Williams hypothesis. Reasoning by an ingenious analogy, David Lewis-Williams, Graham Hancock and others leap-frog this problem. They try to reconstruct the third layer – information on the inner meaning of cave paintings – by going directly to what they claim is its source: revelations transmitted to shaman priests entering and exiting hallucinogenic trance states.[6]

Unfortunately, accounting for the ultimate source -- trance states tuning humanity into a higher dimension where shamans literally saw and continue to see and listen to higher beings – brings us no closer to the inner meaning of these enigmatic cave images, not to mention any nearer to their contextual meaning. The absence of any real explanation for the enigmatic dots prompts Joelle Robert-Lambling to conclude: "[the system of depictions] which comprises not forms but signs, is symbolic and its meaning is still unknown."[7]

Our thesis is that the third layer of meaning cannot be recovered simply by going back in time, the arrow of time prohibits this. And no amount of archeological digging underground or inside prehistoric caves will ever uncover it because *it is not there,* it never was. Only fragments of the literal recording are there, and for this one must express one's gratitude for the tireless efforts of hundreds of men and women beginning with Marcelino Sanz de Sautuola in 1875.[8]

As for the hidden third layer of meaning, it was always in the hearts and souls of shamans and nowhere else, a hidden fountain of cave imagery and direct teaching to initiates in prehistoric times, a fountain returning to its *timeless source* when they died. Only by going outside of time and tapping into this source *directly* can one hope to retrieve the missing layer in our times, *and this is the work of a teacher in an esoteric school connected directly to that source.*[1*] There have

1   * Gurdjieff made it clear to Ouspenskii once the relationship of a teacher and school to this timeless source is not

been many such teachers and schools in the past – ancient Egyptian, Chinese Buddhist, Hindu, Sufi, Hebrew, Medieval Christian. During the 20th century modern successors to those great schools began to appear. One of these, the Fourth Way school of Robert Burton., was destined it seems to recover the hidden inner meaning of those cave paintings. How Burton and his students did this requires a brief discussion of the Fourth Way, its origins, aims and methods.

---

matter of choice or chance. A man in the role of teacher, he observed, "may know more or he may know less about the esoteric [source], he may know exactly where this [source] is and how knowledge and help is received from it; or he may know nothing of this...The results of the work of a [teacher] do not depend on whether or not he knows exactly the origin of what he teaches, but very much depends on whether or not his ideas come *in actual fact* from the [timeless source]

II. For all humanity: a fourth way

The Fourth Way tradition. For tens of thousands, perhaps hundreds of thousands of years, the inner circle of humanity has been receiving, encrypting and decoding divine revelations. The hermetic traditions of pre-historic shaman cave artists, of shaman priests in Ancient Egypt, Sumer, China and India, of the Mosaic and Islamic priests, of the early Desert Fathers, and their successors (Sufis and Cabbalists) grew out of the need to conceal and transmit to future generations this Ancient Teaching. Why conceal it? Why turn secrecy into *a test of will* that continues to this day?

Until quite recently humanity has been fractured into hundreds of local, essentially tribalistic linguistic communities. Warfare has been an ever-present reality, destruction of sacred traditions a constant threat. There was no global linguistic community as there is today, no basis for a gentlemen's agreement to let the sacred traditions of one's enemies co-exist with one's own. For that matter, even today that agreement is fragile at best. Witness the U.S. bombing into oblivion of ancient Sufi temples in Afghanistan -- and now the Russian-krainian War -- presumably on the premise that they were sanctuaries for Al Quaida terrorists, or observe the burning of Buddhists temples in Tibet by the Chinese.

For most of its history then the inner circle of humanity had no choice. It has always had to conceal and hide revelations intended paradoxically for all of humanity. Hermetic encryption was – and for some in the inner circle today –

continues to be a mortal imperative. The leopard has not changed its spots, the snake that poisoned our ancestors yesterday, if you befriend it, still bites.

So what has changed – to justify, for example, this publication? *No one knows for sure.*

For some reason, a generation of spiritual teachers appeared at the turn of the 20th century – Meher Baba, Aleister Crowley, Edgar Cayce, etc. – breaking with the ancient hermetic tradition of silence, and going public. From all traditions spiritually gifted and courageous men and women came forward and began decoding the revelations intended for all of humanity in the first place. Perhaps the reason had something to do with Divine Providence preparing humanity for the devastating psychological shock of two World Wars, the Russian Revolution and its bloody Stalinist aftermath, the Jewish Holocaust and atomic warheads exploding over Hiroshima and Nagasaki. Whatever the reason, the seal of hermetic silence was broken, and remains so to this day.

Among those of that generation breaking with tradition and its code of silence were an Odd Couple -- a luminous-eyed Armenian-Greek and a bespectacled White Russian: Georg Ivanovich Gurdjieff and Peter Ouspenski. In a series of private meetings, public lectures and books spanning nearly a half century these two men and their associates decoded the Sufi, Philokalia and Old Testament/ New Testament teachings in psychological forms they felt would be more understandable to audiences in the West. Sometimes calling these forms *esoteric Christianity,* their system came to be known in the latter half of the 20th century as *the Fourth Way system* or simply *the Fourth Way* *.

A psychology of inner meanings. The Fourth Way is not a system of psychology in the ordinary sense of the word, but in its original sense, that is "a study of the soul" and more significantly, a study of its possibilities. Rich in metaphor and imagery from early 20th century technology - table of hydrogens, food diagrams, buffers, triads, octaves --, the system also has allegories and practices rooted deeply in hermetic traditions thousands of years old.

One allegory tells of a carriage driver parked on the side of a dirt road. Waiting for his Master to return, the sleepy-eyed driver slowly loosens his reins on the horses and drifts into sleep while his horses take advantage of their loosened reins to wander off and graze among the weeds.

Another allegory tells us about the steward of a mansion with many servants. The steward is supervising many house chores more or less at the same time - cleaning, repairing, dusting - preparing for the Master's return.

In both allegories the imagery and storylines are clear, but their inner meaning is not. For thousands of years this has been the signature of hermetic teaching. In this respect, the Fourth Way is no different from previous traditions. But there is a difference, and it comes to this: the seal of hermetic silence was broken by Gurdjieff and his generation, and remains so. The inner meaning of allegories like the two above and, in fact, of all sacred texts, is now viewed as the birthright and property of all humanity, it belongs to no one -- not to us, not to anyone else -- because it belongs to everyone with "a pair of eyes to see and ears to hear".

For this reason, in Chapter IV, *Keys: metaphors across time for the war within* , interested readers will find a brief introduction to hermetic keys, the "eyes" and "ears" for reading and understanding sacred texts. But first, more on the Fourth Way and how we got here.

A practical school. The Fourth Way is not a literary club, it was never intended for those of us who like to theorize and debate both sides of an issue *ad naseum.* And it definitely turns off those of us who prefer to preach rather than practice. Gurdjieff made this clear when he observed: "Many people are convinced that they wish to be free and to know reality, but they do not know the barrier that prevents them from reaching reality.

"They come to me for help, but they are unwilling or unable to pay the price."[11] Gurdjieff was speaking to John Bennett when he observed this, and in a sense it was a photograph of Bennett, but Bennett missed it.[12]

What is the price most of us are unwilling to pay?

It depends on our *chief feature* and the layers of false personality hidden behind this feature. (See *Glossary* for a discussion of chief feature) In the case of Bennett, for example, the price was giving up the illusion that he could take what he had not paid for, that he could teach the Fourth Way without first submitting to the will of Gurdjieff. In the instance of Ouspenski, the price was more fundamental. Ouspenski, it seems, would gladly have paid for *more knowledge,* but not -- we are told -- for *the being* required for that knowledge. Here for Ouspenski at any rate was the chief danger to his work – that he was prepared to increase his level of knowledge without increasing his level of being.[13] Gurdjieff saw this.

In Petrograd in 1916 Gurdjieff sprang a mousetrap: He asked Ouspenski to abandon not only his theory of higher dimensions, but *all of his knowledge up to that point* as a precondition for continuing to receive Gurdjieff's teaching. Understandably, Ouspenski balked. *All his knowledge!*

Gurdjieff insists. What Uspenskii takes to be knowledge, Gurdjieff says, is a mixture of both truth and falsehood. How can one who is asleep discern one from the other? Therefore, *all* had to be burnt. What is genuine, Gurdjieff tells him, would not be burnt.

The force of Gurdjieff's logic drives Uspenskii's back to the wall. Gurdjieff is merciless, he gives him no out, no way to save face. Like a chess master, Gurdjieff's every move has applied just the right amount of pressure at precisely the right time and place.

Finally, after a great struggle, Uspenskii stabilizes and agrees to sacrifice his knowledge. But the cost, in personal terms, is not small. "Naturally," explains Uspenskii, "such submission could not be achieved without great struggle with oneself, and the first results of this was that I entirely lost the power to write."[14]

In both instances (Bennett's and Ouspenski's), the central issue concerned payment for reaching a higher level of being – not payment in the abstract, but *payment by surrendering one's self-will to the will of a teacher.* The system ideas of the Fourth Way, its metaphors, allegories and exercises were crafted to assist in this practical work on being, and for no other reason.

2nd state, 1st state, imagination, negative emotions, identification, buffering, tramp, lunatic, 3rd state, higher centers – these are a few of the system ideas that were introduced to illuminate the ever-changing landscape of our inner being while at the same time revealing its possibilities. This was not simply for the sake of illumination, but so that one might observe and change ones level of being oneself.

In the *Psychology of Man's Possible Evolution* Ouspenski discussed two central ideas – 1) that a man or woman is not just one I – Pytor, Anna, Georg – but many I's and 2) that we exist at different levels of being, each higher level representing a greater degree of unity, will, and consciousness.

The first three levels Ouspenski calls Man No 1, 2 and 3, each representing a pre-dominance of instinctive-moving, emotional and intellectual centers respectively. While quite different functionally, these categories of Man exist at basically the same level of being. [15]

At the level of Man No. 4 something extraordinary happens. Man No. 4 represents a quantum leap of being to a higher level. Men and women at this level, Ouspenski notes, "are not 'born' as such. [They are] a product of school culture." Ouspenski writes:

> [Man No. 4] differs from Man No. 1,2, and 3 by *his knowledge of himself,* by his understanding of his position, and, as it is expressed technically, by his having acquired *a permanent center of gravity.* This last means that the idea of acquiring unity, consciousness, permanent I and will...has already become for him more important than his other interests. Man No. 5 is a *man who has acquired unity and self-cons-ciousness.* He is different from ordinary man because in him *one of the higher centers works*...Man No. 6 is a man who has acquired *objective consciousness. Another higher center works in him*...Man No. 7 is man who has attained all that a man can attain. He has *a permanent I* and *free will.* He can control all the states of consciousness in himself and he already cannot lose anything he has acquired. According to another description, [Man No. 7] is *immortal within the limits of the solar system.* [16]

The crux of all practical work in the Fourth Way: How does one pass from the level of being of Man No. 4 or less to that of Man No. 7? The vocabulary of transition to higher levels of being is quite *short: remember oneself, divide attention, transform suffering, love consciously, be present.* The brevity of this list conceals its extraordinary difficulty, the transition being compared to the difficulty of passing thru a narrow gate or, even worse, the difficulty of a camel passing thru the eye of a needle.

The Institute. In Pera, Russia and two years later at the Prieure in France Gurdjieff experimented with creating a school environment where pupils could work consistently on their four lower centers and, in this way, occasionally experience at least two centers becoming balanced at the same time and presumably allowing pupils to pass thru the narrow gate and connect with higher centers. At the Pera in 1920 Ouspenski assisted Gurdjieff organize the Institute. "The movements and sacred dances are practiced", writes one commentator, "And self-remembering and self-observation are emphasized, as is work with the centers."[17]

Students are told by Gurdjieff that "effort influenced by necessity or desire is no effort. To remember oneself is effort because no external shock can force us. Effort is for the sake of consciousness. Struggle with habits gives a taste of effort. Self-remembering helps balance centers, changes chemical processes and improves nutrition." Students also study the science of numbers, the Cabala, magical arts and the traditions of Asian schools concernng religious myths.

Two years later at the Prieure Gurdjieff organizes the Institute without Ouspenski. By then Ouspenski had broken with Gurdjieff and left the Institute, heading for England to organize his own group. The principle of balancing lower centers to connect with higher centers remains behind with Gurdjieff.

The pupils are put to work scrubbing latrines, felling trees, digging ditches, doing farmwork, gardening, housework, laundry and the like. Everyone is up around four in the morning. Breakfast consists only of coffee, toast and butter...In the evening everyone bathes and dresses for dinner, which is often quite lavish...After dinner Gurdjieff may give a talk, or Thomas de Hartmann play music, or perhaps there are movement [dances]...the physical, emotional and mental demands are great. This unrelenting pressure creates conditions in which students can see themselves – not as they imagine themselves to be, but as they really are.[18]

Lynne Place. What about Ouspenski? Ouspenski moves to London convinced that Gurdjieff's experiment at the Prieure will be a complete failure "simply because the principle of seniority was not followed... People who did not belong to groups before...were given certain power over people who were much older in the Work, it did not work – it could not go on."[19]

After holding private meetings in London for several years, in 1934 Ouspenski moves to Lynne Place, a country estate some twenty miles from London. There Ouspenski begins to host meetings and receive visitors. Meetings are bleak and austere intellectual affairs. No music, no sacred dances, no emphasis on balancing lower functions, only men and women seated in a living room talking and talking and talking -- asking Ouspenski questions and sometimes digesting the shock of his unconventional answers.[20] In the evening after guests are gone, Ouspenski often reminisces over vodka with a few students in the kitchen his days with Gurdjieff.

On the surface at least, Lynne Place seems a complete repudiation of the principles guiding Gurdjieff's Institute. Ignoring superficial differences, however, could it be that Lynne Place became the intellectual negative pole complementing the positively charged, instinctive-moving pole at the Prieure? Is it possible that the separation and divorce of these two remarkable lovers of Truth were necessary payments for a Fourth Way school to appear and arc across time and space and illuminate the inner spiritual darkness of a modern civilization ravaged by World Wars, Bolsehevik and Fascist terrorism, Jewish and nuclear holocausts?

III. All and everything in a pack of cards...

A world-wide movement Ouspenski dies in 1947 from kidney failure induced by alcoholism. Gurdjieff dies two years later, apparently from severe head injuries sustained in an auto accident. At the time of Ouspenski's death there were about 1,000 students in his group and a handful in Gurdjieff's. A half century later the Fourth Way has grown into a world-wide movement of about a dozen 4th Way groups entering the lives and transforming the hearts of tens of thousands of men and women. Gurdjieff's mission to bring the teachings of Sufi masters and Ancient Egyptian Desert Fathers to the West had been fulfilled.

Alexander Horn. A student of Lord Pendleton,[21] Alexander Horn seems to have been the first to use ordinary playing cards to present system ideas related to the four lower centers. At first this may appear to be a trivial innovation, but we will see shortly its momentous consequences for the Fourth Way tradition.

In his Fourth Lecture of *Psychology of Man's Possible Evolution* Ouspensky presents a diagram of the four lower centers. The diagram, Ouspenski explains, represents a man standing sideways and looking to the left. He then reminds us: "*In reality each center occupies the whole body, penetrates, so to speak, the whole organism. At the same time, each center has what is called its "center of gravity".* The center of gravity of the intellectual center is in the brain; The center of gravity of the emotional center is in the solar plexus; The centers of gravity of the moving and instinctive centers are in the spinal cord."[22]

Continuing:

One of the most important principles that must be understood in relation to centers is the great difference in their speed, that is, a difference in the speeds of their functions. The slowest is the intellectual center. Next to it – although very much faster – stand the moving and instinctive centers, which have more or less the same speed. The fastest of all is the emotional center, though in the state of 'waking sleep' [the 2nd state] it works very rarely with anything approximating to its real speed, and generally works with the speed of the instinctive and moving centers.[23]

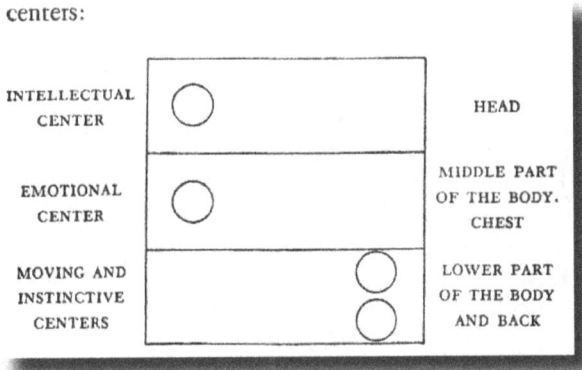

Ouspensky assigns the ratio 30,000:1 to the relative difference in the speeds of centers. Presumably, the moving and instinctive centers are 30,000 times faster than the intellectual center, and the emotional center -- when it "wakes up", connecting to higher centers -- is 30,000 times faster than the instinctive and moving centers.

Is any of this true? We don't know. First of all, no one has ever clocked or can clock the speed of centers   At best one can verify for oneself, for example, that moving and instinctive functions are faster than intellectual functions, and likewise with emotional functions – but all of this happens in the rough, nothing precise.

Horn's innovation cut through the imprecision, reminding us that it does not matter how fast one center is relative to another, what matters is which part of a center one is in. And for this, the visual imagery of playing cards was a stunning gift from the Gods.

Compare the statement: "He's in the emotional part of the intellectual part of the emotional center" to this statement: "He's in the Nine of Hearts." Both statements are saying the same thing, but the first is an opaquetongue-twister; whereas the second is deceptively transparent.

Mapping inner states into cards. Horn succeeded in mapping our inner psychological states in playing cards based on a one-to-one correpondence between each card and each division of the lower centers. In one masterful stroke, playing cards were elevated to *metaphors for the state of the soul.* At the same time, something even more wonderful and profound began to happen quietly below the surface.

Apollo. With their home base in the Sierra foothills about *seventy* miles north of Sacramento and with satellite centers around the world, a generation of students began practicing the Fourth Way in the mid-1970s. Mostly in their twenties, and sometimes teenagers, they literally grew up over a 30-year period using Horn's playing card metaphors to study and work on their psychological states. Guided by Robert Burton, this generation was being prepared it seems for the seismic shock of a revelation re-locating the paradigm for self-remembering to another plane: The ancient hermetic practice of using metaphors to equate one's psychological state to the inner meaning of a sacred text, a poem, painting or event in one's daily life can be coupled to the fourth way practice of remembering oneself. *Playing card imagery became for the first time a simple useful tool for self-observation and photography of the emotional, mental or instinctive-moving state oneself and others are in.*

A war within. Returning to the prehistoric cave paintings and the Egyptian hieroglyphs, their inner meaning turns out not to be missing after all. Hidden for a time, yes, but not missing. For tens of thousands of years it has been where it was in the beginning, and where it is now: inside all of us. With the Table of 72 Functions this inner meaning becomes illuminated like a dark cave, and we see that it is the shifting disposition of a psychological war between two major divisions inside of us – our instinctive center and our emotional center – a war erupting in any of us as soon

TABLE 1 - PLAYING CARD METAPHORS
FOR 72 DIVISIONS OF LOWER CENTERS
AND TWO HIGHER CENTERS
ACES AND KINGS

	DIAMONDS	SPADES	CLUBS	HEARTS
ACES	higher intellectual center			higher emotional center
KINGS	intellectual parts of intellectual center	intellectual parts of moving center	intellectual parts of instinctive center	intellectual parts of emotional center
10	intellectual part of intellectual part of intellectual center	intellectual part of intellectual part of moving center	intellectual part of intellectual part of instinctive center	intellectual part of intellectual part of emotional center
9	emotional part of intellectual part of intellectual center	emotional part of intellectual part of moving center	emotional part of intellectual part of instinctive center	emotional part of intellectual part of emotional center
8	instinctive-moving part of intellectual part of intellectual center	instinctive-moving part of intellectual part of moving center	instinctive-moving part of intellectual part of instinctive center	instinctive-moving part of intellectual part of emotional center

**TABLE 2 - PLAYING CARD METAPHORS
FOR 72 DIVISIONS OF LOWER CENTERS
THE QUEENS**

	DIAMONDS	SPADES	CLUBS	HEARTS
QUEENS	emotional parts of intellectual center	emotional parts of moving center	emotional parts of instinctive center	emotional parts of emotional center
7	intellectual part of emotional part of intellectual center	intellectual part of emotional part of moving center	intellectual part of emotional part of instinctive center	intellectual part of emotional part of emotional center
6	emotional part of emotional part of intellectual center	emotional part of emotional part of moving center	emotional part of emotional part of instinctive center	emotional part of emotional part of emotional center
5	instinctive-moving part of emotional part of intellectual center	instinctive-moving part of emotional part of moving center	instinctive-moving part of emotional part of instinctive center	instinctive-moving part of emotional part of emotional center

40

TABLE 3 - PLAYING CARD METAPHORS
FOR 72 DIVISIONS OF LOWER CENTERS
THE JACKS

	DIAMONDS	SPADES	CLUBS	HEARTS
JACKS	mechanical parts of intellectual center	mechanical parts of moving center	mechanical parts of instinctive center	mechanical parts of mechanical center
4	intellectual part of mechanical part of intellectual center	intellectual part of mechanical part of moving center	intellectual part of mechanical part of instinctive center	intellectual part of mechanical part of emotional center
3	emotional part of mechanical part of intellectual center	emotional part of mechanical part of moving center	emotional part of mechanical part of instinctive center	emotional part of mechanical part of emotional center
2	instinctive-moving part of mechanical part of intellectual center	instinctive-moving part of mechanical part of moving center	instinctive-moving part of mechanical part of instinctive center	instinctive-moving part of mechanical part of emotional center

as we try to awaken and escape the pathetic fate of our biological machines.

"Machines we are born," Gurdjieff once said, "And machines we die." From the beginning, hermetic teachings -- including Gurdjieff's and now Burton's--have been revealing to humanity *how not to die.* And those lessons touch off inner warfare sooner or later.

The combatants. The principal combatants in this war are:

1) *the King of Clubs, a.k.a. the lower self,* 2) *the Nine of Clubs,* 3) *the King of Hearts,* 4) *the Nine of Hearts,* 5) *the steward, and* 6) *higher centers.* Unlike the others, the steward is a product of esoteric schools and their teachings, coming into existence as a direct result of Influence C intervening in our lives and using the Nine of hearts to ignite higher centers. The other biological functions (King of Clubs, King of Diamonds, spades, etc.) are born and develop with the machine. All combatants – King of Clubs, King of Hearts, lower self, steward --, with the exception of higher centers, are fated to die with the machine. And tragically, even higher centers, if they pass thru life stillborn and never awaken in us, finally perish. Without *a second birth* they suffer *the second death* Michelangelo lamented before dying.

Always being waged inside of us, on the scale of the 72 divisions of our machines, the theater of this inner warfare is planetary: Potentially, there could be as many as 6 billion inner wars happening on 72 different fronts. 6 billion times 72, and growing... Unfortunately, there are far fewer. Far, far too few. Why this is so will be discussed shortly.

The weapons: There are *10,000 mechanical I's* appearing in us as imagination, negative emotions, buffers, and features like vanity, greed, power, self-deprecation, dominance, willfulness. To say "in us" is misleading: Usually, we *are* those mechanical I's constantly appearing and then disappearing, about one every few seconds. The King of Clubs uses these I's relentlessly, ruthlessly, mechanically to control the machine.

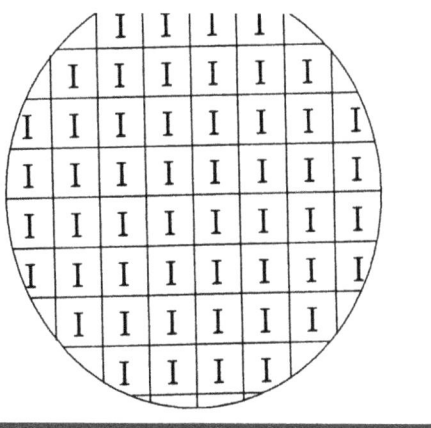

Source, Ouspenski, *Pyschology of Man's Possible Evolution*

Competing with mechanical I's, the weapons of choice for the steward are *Work I's*. At most there are 100 or so -- each one a product of esoteric schools -- appearing in us singularly as efforts to not express negative emotions, to avoid greed, to not self-deprecate, etc. and culminating in brief moments of presence. Work I's are small manifestations of will: *Serve, Kneel, Child, Drop, Be* are just a few of the I's invoked by the steward to combat imagination. The essence of the conflict between the King of Clubs and the steward is precisely this continual zero-sum competition between mechanical I's and Work I's for time, space and energy.

Mechanical I's. The basic unit of perception for any movement, sensation, emotion or thought is called *an I*. An I can be a slow-moving thought from the intellectual center, "1 + 1 = 2", a faster-moving gesture of the arms from the moving center "Turning right!" – or an even faster moving sensation, say, of pain in the instinctive center, "Ouch!" Even faster than this is the speed of I's from the emotional center, "What a beautiful rose." Perceptions from the sex center are even faster. Long before the intellectual center is aware of what has happened, the sex center has registered and acted on the I, "She's pretty."

The examples above demonstrate that our perception of being unified and just one I is an illusion. We are many I's being born and perishing every few seconds: "1 + 1 = 2", "Turning right!", "Ouch!", "What a beautiful rose!", "She's pretty." In fact, over the course of 24 hours, we are thousands of I's. One estimate places the number at about 10,000 a day; and it calls them the 10,000 mechanical I's. If true, that would mean that most of the time we are about 10 mechanical I's coming and going every minute, or about one I every 6 seconds. The 72 divisions of our lower centers represent these 10,000 mechanical I's.

Work I's. What about Work I's? They are not mechanical, they do not come and go in random 3-second bursts over the course of a day. *Work I's are humanity's objective memory of God communicating with us,* instructing us how to ascend the ladder of being and consciousness and enter the Region of Eternal Presence.

More on the main combatants. The King of Clubs we have learned is a metaphor from a deck of playing cards for the instinctive intelligence of the machine. This card controls the allocation of time and energy to each mechanical I. The Ancient Egyptians called it Set (or Seth), meaning literally "stone".

The seat of this intelligence is the Nine of Clubs. Located in the intellectual part of the instinctive center, the Nine of Clubs is responsible for maintaining instinctive homeostasis even at the expense of higher emotional and intellec

tual states. This card is the source of instinctive imagination and 2nd state dreams. The Ancient Egyptians called the Nine of Clubs Apopis, the "Loathsome Worm"; the Sufis called it the lower self.

30,000 times faster than the King of Club, the King of Hearts is another metaphor from playing cards, this time representing the emotional intelligence of our machines. Ancient Egyptians called this intelligence Osiris. Because of its speed, the King of Hearts is invisible to the King of Clubs.[24] The King of Clubs detects the effects of this card, but not the cause.

The seat of the King of Hearts is the Nine of Hearts. Ancient Egyptians had a special name for this seat. Feminizing it, they called her ast, 'the throne". Transliterating ast into Greek, the Ancient Greeks called her Isis. Located in the intellectual part of the emotional center, the Nine of Hearts is responsible for relativity, scale, emotional discrimination and a highly refined emotional energy.

The steward is simply the Nine of Hearts using relativity, scale and discrimination to slowly master the lower self and its 72 divisions and place them at the service of higher centers. Gurdjieff was one of the first to use the metaphor of the steward in its ancient Biblical sense. However, there is an even more ancient Egyptian connection. Being in essence the Nine of Hearts, the steward is Isis wandering the Earth in search of the dismember parts of Osiris, her Beloved.

Starting as an immature, emotionally charged magnetic center in search of the meaning of life, the steward "wanders the Earth" until it finds a school and transforms this "wandering" (read intellectual curiosity of the Queen of Diamonds) into practical work on controlling the lower functions. It becomes Observing I for a while, and then a deputy steward who is able to see the truth and discriminate between imagination and presence, but unable to do anything about it.

At a more advanced stage, the steward is mature enough to see things as they are, itself as it is, to avoid imagination and be present to its nothingness and that of everything else around it.

The mature steward discovers the real meaning of life in ecstatic remembrance of its higher self (higher centers) and Influence C, in serving them and nothing else. The steward is no longer Isis, trying to remember herself, but radiant Horus, bird-man of purified fire igniting higher centers.

Higher centers. The less said about this mysterious pair, the better since discussing them invites lying. Suffice it to say, presence is a higher emotion ignited under grace by the efforts of a steward mature enough to work on will, it is also a higher intelligence emerging from seeing the (right) hand of Influence C in everything, especially work on will, and in some mysterious way becoming that hand.

How the war begins. The war begins only when Influence C intervenes in our lives collecting what seem random accidental bits and pieces of Influence B and A (but are neither random nor accidental) into a magnetic center "wandering the earth", and this erupts into open warfare when one's magnetic center finds a school and its wandering ends. Until then there is no warfare, no conflict, only the blissful illusion of harmony and peace because there is no steward, no higher centers igniting, only imagination, an endless uninterrupted stream of mechanical I's and our King of Clubs in uncontested control.

How can there be war when one of the adver-saries is asleep?.

This explains why the number of inner wars happening on the planet is infinitesimally smaller than 6 billion times 72. How many? Who knows. Order of magnitude? Try 6,000 psychological wars on 72 fronts, sometimes growing, sometimes shrinking. 6,000 out of 6 billion. To put it mildly, the odds against humanity escaping are terrifying.

But after the steward begins to work on itself a strange war begins, more like a deadly Belgian Cake Walk: The steward takes two steps forward, not expressing a negative emotion and destroying a stream of mechanical I's with the simple Work I: Be! Be? Not seeing the steward because of its speed, the King of Clubs sees only the paralyzing effects of Be on mechanical I's and takes one step back, giving a burst of energy to greed feature and letting a group of mechanical I's explode with negativity and destroy the Work I.

Taking three steps forward and turning to the right, the steward responds fearlessly with more Work I's: Be, Hold, Gods. Puzzled by this stream of strange I's serving no useful instinctive function, the King of Clubs takes two steps back turning to the left with self deprecation and blasphemous I's: Who are you? There is no God. The steward responds: Back!

How it ends. The war between the two major divisions of our machines – the King of Clubs and its allies, the Nine of Heart's steward and its Work I's -- continues intermittently in this fashion for hours, days months, years with casualties, losses and defections on both sides. And let's be honest: Were it not for grace – the outside help of Influence C intervening when it chooses to tip the scale toward the heavily outnumbered steward (remember the ratio of mechanical I's to Work I's is about 100 to 1) -- the King of Clubs would triumph.

But sooner or later even this too must pass. The war ends, we die, and either our death is not only a death of the machine, but a second death if the King of Clubs has won, meaning the still born death of higher centers. Or the war ends at some point in a second birth, meaning the igniting of higher centers by the steward before it dies, a birth that can happen even before our physical death.

The missing layer of meaning revisited. This then is what the missing layer of meaning in prehistoric cave images at Chauvet, Altimira and elsewhere is about, fragmentary notwithstanding: the ongoing psychological war inside any of us seeking to escape. For that matter, any painting or inscription of any significance in prehistoric caves, in temple ruins, any work of art, both religious and secular, all the great sacred writings treasured and fought over, all the great philosophical works read by us now or destroyed, and all the secular writings -- all of these are treating one or more aspects of this war. Otherwise whatever is being painted, written or put to music is Shakespeare's "tale told by an idiot, full of sound and fury, signifying nothing."

IV. Keys: metaphors across time for the war within

"All that Ouspensky said and did at that time seemed to me to have exactly this purpose and effect - to sort out the people who could respond to the miraculous from those who could not, and also to sort out in these people themselves the small part which could respond from the large part which was unable to do so."

Rodney Collin, Theory of Conscious Harmony

Keys to the Fourth Way: Robert Burton and his students were fated, it seems, to re-discover keys, those ancient missing links connecting the contextual meaning of anything -- a pre-historic cave image, a Shakespeare sonnet, a Rembrandt painting, a sacred text, a palm tree, a rose -- to the inner psychological warfare raging inside those of us trying to escape. Keys are reminders of this war, reminders of the combatants, the theater, the weapons and the stakes (second birth or a second death). Ouspenski and Gurdjieff were looking for keys, but did not find them.[25] Looking for evidence of the fourth way in sacred texts, Burton found keys. Everywhere.[262]

2   * One is reminded of the Sufi story of a drunk man looking for his keys under a lamppost in darkness. Coming out of the tavern, a fellow drinker looks on sympathetically as his dear friend bends over in the light of the lamppost, squinting and staring without result at the ground under his feet. "What are you looking for, my friend", the sympathetic onlooker asks. "My keys, my keys!" the drunkard answers. "Did you lose them under the lamppost?" his friend asks innocently. Looking up for a moment, the drunkard replies: "No, but this is where the light is." The keys to hermetic knowledge could never be found in the darkness (read A-Influence), not because they are hidden there somewhere, and nobody can find them, but because the

Mapping the Bible. It began innocently enough, with a series of weekly Bible studies in 2003: A close reading of the Old and New Testaments brought Robert Burton and his secretary Asaf Braverman to several revelations:

1)   The words "God" and "Lord" not only have a literal meaning, but an inner psychological meaning immediately recognizable to students of the Fourth Way. "God" and "Lord" also mean higher centers, divine presence.

2)   The list of prophets and heroes from Moses to Jesus and including David, Solomon, Peter and John are different names for that part of the Nine of Hearts discriminating and controlling lower centers called the steward.

3)   The Ten Commandments and the Lord's Prayer are, in fact, Work I's giving the steward instructions for engaging and prolonging presence.

4)   The list of biblical women including Eve, Sara, Ruth, Mary Mother of Jesus and Mary Magdalene are different names for the Nine of Hearts.

5)   The serpent in the Garden of Eden, the Pharaohs

---

keys are the light itself, the ancient hermetic teaching distilled by Gurdjieff and Ouspenski into the fourth way. Using this light -- the light of fourth way knowledge -- to search for keys, Burton found them *everywhere* because they are the light. Like a relativistic physicist, he found what he was looking for in what he was looking with.

persecuting Jews in captivity and pursuing Moses (but not the earlier Pharaoh elevating Joseph to a Vizier), Judas, and the Satan tempting Jesus are different names for the King of Clubs.

6)   "Good" means anything promoting presence or simply being present, and "evil" means anything promoting imagi-nation or simply being in imagination.

Gurdjieff's two allegories revisited. With Burton's keys, let's return to Gurdjieff's two allegories. What do they mean?

As you recall, the first allegory tells of a carriage driver parked on the side of a dirt road. Waiting for his Master to return to the carriage, the sleepy-eyed driver slowly loosens his reins on the horses and drifts into sleep while his horses take advantage of their loosened reins to wander off and graze among weeds.

What is the inner meaning of this story so transparently clear at the literal level? In Burton's system of keys "carriage driver" is a key for the steward and "Master" a key for higher centers. "Loosening his reins" is a key for the steward losing control of lower centers, "horses" represent the four lower centers. "Sleep" is identification and "grazing among weeds" a key for slipping into imagination.

The hidden meaning of this allegory now becomes transparent: Sometimes the steward drifts off into such a deep state of identification that the lower centers slip into imagination. Nothing earthshaking, simple, and yet capable of producing a small shock of presence.

The second allegory tells us about the steward of a mansion

with many servants. The steward is supervising many house chores more or less at the same time – cleaning, repairing, dusting – preparing for the Master's return. "Mansion" is a key for the Nine of Hearts; "servants" a key for Work I's, "cleaning" for purifying the Nine of Hearts, "repairing" for healing and "dusting" for ridding the emotional center of imagination.

The inner meaning of this second allegory is also simple: The steward prepares the emotional center for re-connecting to higher centers by using Work I's which purify and heal the Nine of Hearts. At the same time, it uses other Work I's to keep the emotional center out of imagination.

An Invariance Principle. Cabalists reading the above may be unimpressed, observing that they have been decoding Biblical allegories for hundreds of years in this way. So where is the innovation, they ask? First, it is in linking the inner meaning of the Old and New Testaments to the psychological structures and states described in the 4th Way, thus creating a context for conscious shocks, that is, shocks that produce presence by design. But secondly, Influence-C did not let matters rest there. Burton's vision transcends Biblical exegesis, Cabalist and otherwise. He insists that true keys must apply across the board to all sacred literature and art – Buddhist, Islamic, Ancient Greek, Chinese, Hindu –, and not just to Judaeo-Christian art.

Now this can mean only one of two things: EITHER keys are culturally local linguistic events and vary from civilization to civilization and time period to time period, and Burton is wrong. Every civilization and age has to discover its own unique set of keys. OR Influence C has been transmitting through Burton and other spiritual teachers the same message for hundreds of thousands of years: The inner meaning of sacred texts, art, and music is invariant across civilizations and time periods, and always has been. Influence C is transmitting to all of us the same message: human suffering, love, the mystery of grace, transcendence and ultimate redemp-tion.

First invariance test: Egyptian hieroglyphs. As you recall, we stopped short of keying the hieroglyph ua, "number one of the Gods." Our reasoning then was straight-forward: We felt we did not have the mapping algorithm the Ancient Egyptians used for encrypting this hieroglyph. But now the Invariance Principle tells us that, in a
sense, we do have it: The harpoon image is the clue. Literally, it means "that which pierces", and it turns out this is a key for Short Be, the first Work I in a sequence of Work I's, its task: to pierce and dispel imagination.

Short Be. Linguistically, the words "Short Be" go against the grain of the logical formatory mind. The logic of this mind runs like this: "No one proficient in English would ever use "Be" that way. And to call it "Short" only height-ens the absurdity."

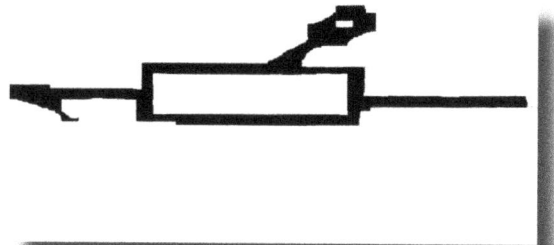

The fallacy of formatory logic is its insistence on confin-ing English to the narrow limits of our everyday usage, and Burton is doing precisely the opposite: Pushing ordinary English (the profane) beyond these limits to remind us of the miracle of presence in our midst (the sacred). No wonder the confusion.

Burton is not the first to do this nor will he be the last. Rumi and other Sufi masters pushed the envelop of Persian with this very word, Be. Likewise Rilke with Sein, and Gurdjieff with the neologisms he invented in Beelzebub's Tales to the consternation of his generation and ours imitating Ancient Egyptian. Burton has simply taken this a step further:

There is not just one state of presence, Burton explains, but three. First, there is a state of presence whose signature is the steward manifesting will by interrupting the flow of mechanical I's and replacing it briefly with a Work I. Burton calls this act of will Short Be. Without it the steward would remain trapped in imagination, a sequence could not begin, higher centers would more than likely pass through this life stillborn, no second birth.[3]

Middle Be. States of presence have another general form captured in the everyday expression presence of mind. In moments like this the degree of presence is measured by the steward's relative success or failure in controlling the 72 divisions of centers Burton calls the lower self. Recall that the steward is simply the Nine of Hearts (the intellectual brain "inside" our emotional center) using relativity, scale and discrimination to calm down and eventually educate the lower self. Burton calls this second form of presence Middle Be, shorthand for the steward manifesting

---

3   ¨ Here we are dealing with probabilities. Even without sequences, outside help in the form of shocks directly from Influence C is always possible, meaning second births without prayer sequences always remain mathematically possible, they are just less likely than continual sleep that's all.

sufficient "presence of mind" (usually midway through a sequence) to control its (lower) self.

Long BE. In our 2nd example, we discovered that the hieroglyph aft for the number four has associations with two and three dimensional objects (rectangular boxes and sarcophagus). The inner meaning of this association would remain hidden without keys. With Burton's keys, however, we discover two related meanings: At the end of every sequence of Work I's there is a 6th Work I called Long BE – the third form of presence. Also, we have learned from Burton that boxes, coffins and sarcophagi are metaphors for this Work I.

After completing a sequence and reaching Long BE, Burton advises students to take four breaths (metaphorically this author thinks, others are more literal-minded)– four inhalations and exha- lations -- to prolong the this third form of presence. In this context, Burton associates the number four with these breaths, calling them four wordless breaths.

What is Long BE?

Long BE is more hermetic shorthand, more of the profane

being used to remind us of the sacred, this time to remind us of the mystery of a presence transcending the steward's efforts to be present – transcending, that is, both its acts of will in Short Be and its moment of presence in Middle Be mastering its lower self. In this moment of transcendence the steward's work is done, it has temporarily pierced the veil of imagination, its lower self is momentarily under control. Now it itself must step aside briefly and let higher centers be present. Metaphorically the steward has to die. That is why Burton associates Long BE with the imagery of coffins, boxes (side view of a coffin), squares (end view of a box), sarcophagi.

Purifying the Nine of Hearts. The steward is no saint, our Nine of Hearts no virgin. That is why sequences are necessary: They are designed to purify our lower emotional center in preparation for higher centers. In the three forms of presence discussed above what might otherwise seem incomprehensible madness to the logical mind falls into place revealing with amazing clarity and precision the recurrent structure of prayer – Short Be interrupting imagination at the beginning, Middle Be keeping the lower self in check at the interval, and at the end Long BE connecting the Nine of Hearts to higher centers. No matter the specific form – Buddhist mantra, Christian prayer beads, Jesus prayer, Jewish proverb, Sufi love poem – all forms of prayer have this structure, it is invariant across civilizations, religions and time.

Returning to the hieroglyph for the number six, perhaps its association with "six-threaded garment" and "6th day of the festival of purification", depending on the determinative, is less enigmatic. Beginning with the number six itself, by association it is a key for the six Work I's in a sequence. "Six-threaded garment" is a key for the sequence itself, and "6th day of the festival of purification" a key for the moment when higher centers connect with a purified Nine of Hearts and are present at Long BE.

A radiant presence. In our final sample hieroglyph, aaku, its hidden meaning was not lost, it seems. The principle of invariance permits us to recover this layer from the hieroglyph's literal and contextual meanings. At the literal level, the determinative is imagery without phonetic value and consists of three rays of light pouring out of a sun disk . While this is our main clue, the various contextual meanings of aaku– radiant being of light, light itself, beautiful deeds, splendid acts, virtues and blessings – narrow the hieroglyph's inner meaning to one candidate: presence of higher centers.

The source of invariance. Since it's simmering in the background, let's put invariance on the front burner and turn up the heat: A sympathetic skeptic: "You may be on to something here, but is this invariance business really

necessary? I mean what's so terrible about each hermetic tradition having its own set of keys and inner meanings? If, in the end, it's about producing shocks that promote presence, what difference does it make which hidden meaning does this?"

One answer: One's level of being and consciousness makes the difference. At our level – that of Men No. 1, 2, 3, or 4 perhaps -- it doesn't seem to make much difference, but at the level of being of Ibn Arabi, Bahauiddin, Rumi, Bernard of Clairvaux, Gurdjieff, Meher Baba, Alexander Horn, and last, but not least, Robert Burton a set of universal meanings cutting across all traditions and uniting them is a self-evident, completely verifiable truth.

How is that possible?

According to one theory, at their level of being, the inner circle of humanity is experiencing direct and continuous communication with a region of divine intelligence Gurdjieff calls Influence C. Thru these men and women a timeless teaching with its own dictionary of higher connections is being transmitted to humanity all the time from this region, and this has been the case ever since humanity came into existence. It has never changed in content or implication even though its imagery and form have changed. The same now as it was thousands of years ago, this sacred teaching is the objective collective memory of a divine intelligence communicating with the inner circle of humanity, a memory which is not personal, it is not mine, not yours, and it remains the same whether it is being received in Tibet, India or New York City.

Is this theory true?

We have no way of knowing this side of igniting our own higher centers and becoming conscious. What we do know for sure is that Burton and others are insistent on the principle of invariance. It anchors the inner meaning of sacred texts, works of art, even science itself in a timeless objective memory, reminding us it is still the same even though its outer form and imagery have changed across civilizations and over time.

2nd test: prehistoric cave paintings. The most difficult test now faces us: retrieving the third layer of meaning from prehistoric rock art. Our efforts earlier demonstrated, it is hoped, that without hermetic keys the recovery task is impossible. The discussion above of an invariance principle operating across civilizations and time has prepared us for the following shock: the third layer of meaning, the inner layer hidden for thousands of years, was never lost, it has always been a part of humanity's collective memory.

What has been missing sometimes, what has been coming and going like the morning dew over tens of thousands of years, are men and women at a level of being and consciousness advanced enough to tune into this memory at will. This author is convinced Robert is one of those rare and gifted individuals.

Red dots revisited. Returning to the enigmatic red dots at Chauvet: On one wall there are six, next to three red vertical lines and a horse's head outlined in yellow with one vertical line below it. On another wall there are ten. Dots and vertical lines are some of our earliest examples of counting numbers, six, three and ten, which Burton has keyed: Six is a key for the six Work I's of a sequence; three a key for the three states of being of the steward during a sequence Ten dots keys the sequence of six Work I's, followed by four wordless breaths (6+4=10).

Look carefully at the painting of six red dots. Besides the three vertical lines, one can make out the figure of an animal outlined just above them. There is also one vertical line under the horse head. Could this be one of the earliest examples of the method of counting used in ancient Egyptian hieroglyphs?

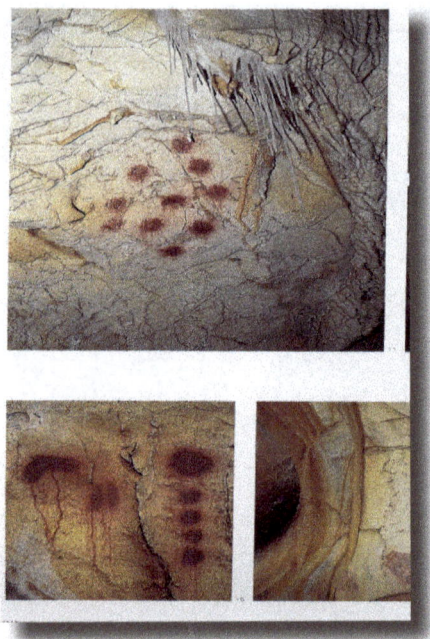

For comparison, look again at the hieroglyphs for three, four and six. Observe the vertical lines positioned sometimes just below a determinative. A coincidence? Maybe not. Perhaps this is evidence for a counting tradition tens of thousands of years old. Put differently, perhaps our first hieroglyphs are to be found not only inside Chauvet, Lescaux and other pre-historic European cave sites, but in caves even older than Chauvet and buried perhaps under the sands of the Sahara or even more likely to be found in South Africa among the rock art of the ancient Sans culture.

GLOSSARY

Be - a one syllable invocation to "be present", meaning "come out of imagination". There are two forms -- Short Be corresponding to the Egyptian hieroglyph un and Long BE corresponding to the hieroglyph au. Coming at the start of a sequence, Short Be pierces the veil of imagination. Coming at the end, Long BE prolongs the state of presence created by the sequence. Metaphors for Short Be are the Red Crown and Isis. Metaphors for Long BE are the White Crown, Osiris in himummy state, and the vulture. Short Be's sacred number is one. Long BE's is six.

Book of Day - a companion sacred text to the Amduat. In the same way that the Amduat traces Re's journey through the night (the 2nd state), the Book of Day is tracing Ra's journey through the day from dawn to sunset (the 3rd and 4th states of presence). Unlike the Amduat, instead of having a painting for each hour, the Book of Day depicts all twelve hours in one painting. This means twelve barks of Ra are depicted, and twelve sun disks. Metaphorically, the Book of Day is transcribing higher centers journey from the 3rd state at dawn (Short Be) to the 4th state at noon (Middle Be) back to the 3rd state at sunset (the Long BE of presence). Written more or less at the same time as the Amduat (15th century BC), the Book of Day employs the same imagery, style and syntax, thus suggesting a common author. The names of nine of the 12 daylight hours are (hours 3,4, and 5 are missing):

1ST HOUR: She Who Lifts Up the Beauty of Ra (SUNRISE)
2nd HOUR: She Who Disperses Darkness
- 3 missing hours --
6th HOUR: The Portal Who Seizes (NOON)
7th HOUR: She Who Gives Joy
8th HOUR: Jubilation
9th HOUR: - described, but unnamed
10th HOUR: She Who Lights the Sky
11th HOUR: Beautiful Sight
12th HOUR: She Who Gives Light in the Island of Life (SUNSET)

broken sequence – Sequences are a special class of ascending octaves. They ascend in order to connect the Nine of Hearts with higher centers. At any point in this ascent sequences may turn into their opposite, they can "lose their wings" and begin to descend, dragging the steward deeper into imagination. When this happens, the octave is called a broken sequence. Usually this happens at the 4th and 6th steps of a sequence. Since they are ascending, sequences require extraordinary amounts of sex energy. At steps 4 and 6 the energy available for completing a sequence drops off. Why this happens is still unclear. We know that between the 3rd and 4th steps the steward passes thru a mi-fa interval, and again, during the 6th step, when it passes thru a si-do. We know that much, what we do not know is why the sequence slows down in these intervals in the first place.

buffer - a defense mechanism the emotional center creates to protect itself from emotionally traumatic events. Usually in some state of imagination when it creates a buffer, the emo-tional center inserts it between memories of two related emotional events, Like padding between railcar couplers, the defense mechanism is called a buffer because it prevents two contradictory events, often emotionally charged, from colliding and being remembered simultaneously. When remembered together, contradictory memories often cause acute emotional anxiety up to and sometimes including psychotic breaks. The main property of buffers is their invisibility, a person is completely unaware the buffer exists even when his emotional center is using it to "keep up appearances".

centers (of gravity) In the Fourth Lecture of his Psychology of Man's Possible Evolution, written in 1934, and the text for a series of lectures attracting thousands in London, Ouspensky presented a schematic box diagram of a man standing sideways to illustrate the principle of the sixfold division of the soul. He called each division a center of gravity or simply a center, one center for intellectual activity, a second for moving or motor-sensory activity, a third for instinctive and a fourth for emotional perceptions. Collectively, he called these the four lower centers and did so to sharply differentiate them from a pair of activities he called higher emotional and higher intellectual centers or simply higher centers. (not shown on the diagram) These higher centers are the seat of revelations, mystical dreams, even mathematical and scientific discoveries.

chief feature - There are 72 divisions of the machine, each representing a negative or positive part of the five lower centers, and manifesting itself as a group of habitually recurring mechanical I's we call features. Among these habitually recurring I's there is one group that dominates and influences the others, this group is called chief feature. Usually tending to too much relativity (tramp) or too little (lunatic feature), chief feature reflects not just one's center of gravity but one's body type and alchemy.

combustion - The higher emotional center (World 12) has to be ignited before there can be presence. The purpose of sequences is to assist the steward do precisely that: ignite higher centers. Starting with Short Be and ending with Long BE and the 4 wordless breaths, this process is called combustion. In a sense, the sequence is the match, higher emotional center the flammable material, and the steward the striker. Red is the color code for combustion.

four wordless breaths - a metaphor for the steward prolonging presence at Long BE and igniting higher emotional center.

Fourth Way. The most recent addition to hermetic teachings, based on the teachings of Georg Gurdjieff and Peter Ouspenski, with roots in Sufi teachings, the Philakalia, and ancient Egyptian mystery schools. Fourth Way refers to one of the four ways. According to Gurdjieff, these are: 1) the way of the fakir based on strengthening the intellectual part of the instinctive-moving center, 2) the way of the monk based on strengthening the intellectual part of the emotional center, 3) the way of the yogi based on
strengthening the intellectual part of the intellectual center, and 4) the fourth way based on using the other three ways to balance the intellectual parts of the lower centers. With the aroma of something eclectic, the fourth way is, in fact, a calculated synthesis, a unity designed to be not only greater than the sum of its three parts, but "uncloudy", precise and objective enough to ensnare the hearts and minds of a skeptical, scientifically-trained 21st-century audience.

higher centers - Being the seat of presence, the higher emotional and higher intellectual centers are responsible for 3rd and 4th states. Conscience, the emotional perception of truth, self-remembering, are properties of higher emotions (World 12). Revelations, visionary dreams, interpretation of dreams, prophecies are properties of higher intellectual center (World 6). Their synonym is divine presence, their names the God Within, God, Lord, Third Eye, Eye of Ra, Eye of Horus. Metaphors for higher centers include the sun, the ace of hearts for higher emotions and the ace of diamonds for higher intelligence.

hermetic - refers to anything alchemical, magical, or astrological. Hermetic texts are usually subdivided into the philosophical and technical hermetica. The former deals mainly with issues of philosophy, and the latter with magic, potions and alchemy. In The Emerald Tablet, a short work attributed to Hermes Trismegistus, one finds the famous maxim "As above, so below." The actual text of that maxim, as translated by Dennis W. Hauck, is "That which is Below corresponds to that which is Above, and that which is Above corresponds to that which is Below, to accomplish the miracle of the One."

higher self - another name for higher centers, emotionally warm, self-sacrificing, loving, in a state of ecstasy.

imagination - Every 6 seconds an I is born and perishes mechanically inside one of the 72 divisions of our biological machine. Since there are 24 x 60 mins. x 60 seconds in a day, this means there about 24 x 600 = 14,000 I's being born and perishing mechanically each day. About 4,000 of these come and go when we are in first state (In the text, the estimate for mechanical I's in the 2nd state has been rounded to 10,000) This continual cacophony of emotional, intellect-tual and instinctive/moving- centered perceptions jumping into and out of existence like free electrons creates the illusion of a single unified I, of unity and permanence of thought, emotion and feeling. The illusion is called imagination and consists of a continual stream of I's, one mechanical I coming into existence and wearing the crown of being (an illusion) for six seconds only to be replaced through free association by another mechanical I. A treadmill of mechanical I's without unity, without permanence, without reality. Metaphors for imagination are mountain, water, weeds, sea, clouds, Inferno, Hell, Wheel of Fortune, treadmill.

Influence C – a clinical description for God (higher centers) communicating directly with humanity (the steward and Nine of Hearts) through divine revelation, miracles, divine intervention, wordless shocks, conscious teachers and esoteric schools, past and present. Synonyms: objective memory of humanity, World 6 and World 12. These "influences" are contrasted with B-Influence (sacred texts, sacred art and architecture, lectures, books like this one) documenting Influence C's existence in music, song, poetry, the visual and plastic arts.

The signature of true Influence B is that it always points to Influence C. Influence C and B are both put in sharp contrast to Influence A, representing everything devoted directly or indirectly to perpetuating humanity's biological existence, including the King of Clubs inside each one of us, our biological families, our pursuit of professions, programming of the 72 passions at home and school. Gurdjieff coined the clinical terms A, B, and C-Influence as part of a strategy to make the ancient hermetic teaching more accessible to the West.

inhaling / exhaling 4 wordless breaths - a moving-centered metaphor for the steward prolonging presence at Long BE and igniting higher emotional center. Eight is the sacred number for this state.

intellectual parts of centers - Our biological machines have five lower centers and two higher centers. Each lower center is further divided into three parts -- an intellectual part, an emotional and instinctive parts, with each of these parts being subdivided into negative and positive halves. Intellectual parts of centers refers to the intellectual part of the major division of a center. In terms of Alexander Horn's playing card metaphors, the 10's, 7's, and 4's of each suite, both negative and positive. Other metaphors: men, hands, feet, arms, legs.

Long BE - a one-syllable Work I invoked at the end of a sequence to prolong presence. Metaphors: the White Crown, the vulture, evening star in the West, 4 wordless breaths. Sacred number: 6.

lower centers - The five divisions of our biological machines are: intellectual center, moving center, instinctive center, emotional center and sex center. These are also sometimes called the lower centers in contrast to two other centers: the higher emotional and higher intellectual centers.

lower self - the center of gravity of the five lower centers, the axis around which all the mechanical I's issuing from the five divisions turn. Cold, calculating, unemotional, also called the King of Clubs

King of Clubs - a metaphor from a deck of playing cards signifying the intellectual part of the instinctive center, the seat of the biological machine's instinctive intelligence. Synonym: lower self. Its associated metaphors: serpent, Set, Judas, Apopis, hippopotamus, Satan, whale

King of Hearts - a metaphor from a deck of playing cards signifying the seat of the biological machine's emotional intelligence. Its associated metaphor: The White King in chess.

mechanical I - another name for a unit of perception. Based on the velocity of each perception (about one every 6 seconds) there are roughly 14,000 mechanical I's a day, a spinning wheel of emotional, intellectual, instinctive, moving-centered I's jumping into and out of existence like free electrons, creating the illusion of a single unified I. Its metaphor: cackling geese. Whenever a mechanical I promotes negative imagination, devil and demon are appropriate metaphors.

metaphor - a direct comparison between two or more seemingly unrelated subjects that typically uses "is a" or "is the" to join the subjects and open a window of hidden meaning. Thus, the Soul is the King of Hearts, and the King of Hearts is the intellectual part of the emotional center. A metaphor is commonly confused with a simile, which compares two subjects using "like" or "as". An example of a simile: "He was as sly as a fox." Metaphor is direct: "He is a sly fox." Originally, metaphor was a Greek word meaning "to carry or transfer from here to there".

Nine of Clubs - a metaphor from a deck of playing cards for the seat of instinctive intelligence, located in the intellectual part of the instinctive center, responsible for maintaining instinctive homeostasis even at the expense of higher emotional and intellectual states, source of instinctive imagination and 2nd state dreams.

Nine of Hearts - a metaphor from a deck of playing cards for the site of emotional intelligence in the intellectual part of the emotional center, responsible for relativity, scale and emotional discrimination, the seat of the soul called by Ancient Egyptians "the narrow gate" and by Gurdjieff and Ouspensky "the steward". Associated metaphors: boat, house, mansion, temple, earth, palm tree, rosebush, grapevine, lotus flower, carriage, coffin, sarcophagus, burning bush

octave - Originally referring to the eight natural notes in a twelve tone scale having the interesting property that there are two points in the scale when the pitch frequencies slow down -- namely a mi-fa interval between the 3rd and 4th notes and a si-do between the 7th and 8th. Gurdjieff generalized this property into the Law of 7 or Law of Octaves: Everything ascending, without exception, has to first pass through a mi-fa interval and then, if it bridges the interval, through a si-do interval to reach a higher octave of being. Without exception, all the time. The corollary: if one does not bridge the first or second interval, the ascent is broken off, and one descends. One enters a new, descending octave, passing quickly thru its si-do and then descending slowly like Alice in the rabbit hole to a lower mi-fa, only to drop abruptly into the do of a newer, even lower octave of being

presence - 3rd and 4th states of higher centers beyond words. Metaphors: the color blue, a blue sky, sunlight, day.

purification - the process of the steward using a sequence of Work I's to momentarily interrupt the stream of associative mechanical I's in the Nine of Hearts called imagination (see imagination) and create a moment of presence. Color: white

sequence - an octave ascending in 6 steps, and not 8, but retaining all the properties of an 8-note ascending octave: recurrence of steps, movement to higher levels, intervals, the breaking of ascent at the intervals if not enough intelligent efforts are made. Until the 6th step octaves and sequences are identical. But at the 6th step something remarkable happens: The sequence stretches its 6th step to include the last three notes of the octave – A, B, C or LA, SI, DO – plus the si-do interval. That is why this sixth step is called Long BE: it covers a distance at least three times as long as the first step (called Short Be) and on top of that it includes an interval. The si-do interval hidden inside the 6th step is the reason this step is hazardous. (In the Amduat Ancient Egyptians call this step humorously "Boat That Capsizes") Metaphors for sequence: pyramid, mountain of God, rope, staff, doorway, narrow gate, eye of the needle.

Short Be - a one-syllable Work I invoked at the beginning of a sequence to pierce the veil of imagination, i.e., interrupt the stream of associative, mechanical 6-second I's. Its metaphor: the morning star in the East, the Red Crown combusting. Its sacred number: one.

steward - the Nine of Hearts using its relativity, scale and discrimination to slowly master the lower self and its 72 divisions and place them at the service of higher centers. Starting as an immature emotionally charged magnetic center in search of the meaning of life, the steward finding a school transforms this search into practical work on controlling the lower functions. It becomes Observing I, and then deputy steward able to see the truth, but unable to do anything about it. At a more advanced stage, the steward is mature enough to see things as they are, itself as it is, that it is a nothingness like everything else around it, that the real meaning of life, its crowning achievement, is to live each moment in remembrance of God and Influence C, and simply be present to this.

The steward's methods for reaching this state include using sequences, invoking presence of higher centers directly with Be, Peace, Gods. Its task: to turn the wild hippopotamus inside lower centers into the Bull Without A Halo on Tarot Card 21, to turn the Set inside that tears out Horus Left Eye in the Pyramid Texts into the Set that stands alongside Isis in the 7th Hour of the Amduat using magic to defend Ra from Apopis. Its metaphors: all the historical prophets and heroes of myth: Horus, Joseph, Moses, David, Solomon, Buddha, Jesus, Odysseus, Mohammed, Lao Tze, Arjuna. Animal metaphors: hawk, Anubis, Thoth, dung beetle. The steward is a product of work on oneself in an esoteric school.

Work I - a unit of perception, usually in the intellectual or emotional center and based on the Teaching. Examples of Work I's: "be present", "set noble aims", "Soul", "awaken to the higher reality", "God", "the Soul longs for God", "biological machine", "scale and relativity", "higher reality", "Nine of Hearts", "King of Clubs", "lower self". Metaphors: 30-foot spear, bows, arrows, sword, whip, garments, stars, grass, grapes, palm leaves.

APPENDIX A Sufi and Cabbalist Traditions

The Sufi tradition. Sufism represents a fusion of Islamic and Neo-Platonic teachings. Its hermitic forms are based on the premise that the essence of God is hidden, and not just unknowable but so unknowable it cannot even be imagined, no like, no opposite. His names and attributes, on the other hand, are knowable, and this knowledge becomes the basis for metaphor and allegory.

Rumi, for example, uses the metaphor of the sun for God's presence: "everlasting, no yesterday", neither rising or setting . As for the names of God, they are not simply proper names with a phonetic value, but attributes for example of 1) number: the one (tawhid), oneness of being (wahdatu'l-wujud), 2) life -- basir (seeing with presence), sami (hearing with presence), alim (knowing with presence), jabbar (all powerful), 3) time and space -- asl-awwal (First), al-akhir (Last), al-batin (inner), al-zahir (outer) Other metaphors: circle, light, divine Eye, cloud, stars, breath, inhalation, exhalation.

Making the division into literal, allegorical and inner meanings, the Sufi tradition goes further. In the Masnavi Rumi explains how there is a fourth level of meaning hidden within the third, a fifth within the fourth, and so on up to seven levels of inner meaning, all beyond words and images.

The Cabbala tradition. To begin with, Hebrew scriptures are written without vowels, punctuation or spacing -- much like Egyptian hieroglyphs. Because of this there is always uncertainty about the pronunciation. Since Hebrew has no separate glyphs representing numerical values, letter can represent either a number or a letter. Numerology becomes an integral property of sacred writing.

Rabbi Bahya ben Asher writing in the 13th century wrote: "The Scroll of the Torah is [written] without vowels, in order to enable man to interpret it however he wishes - as the consonants without the vowels bear several interpretations and [may be] divided into several sparks. This is the reason why we do not write the vowels of the scroll of the Torah, for the significance of each word is in accordance with is vocalization, but when it is vocalized it has but one single significance; but without vowels man may interpret it [extrapolating from it] several [different] things, many, marvelous and sublime."

One commentator notes: "Instead of a fixed meaning the scriptures were viewed as having a dynamic meaning, whose actual meaning depended upon the relation between a person and God. Thus the reading of the scriptures was considered a dynamic affair, literally a type of creation in which divine potencies were brought to light as meanings were created in the relation of man to God through the text."

An 18th century Rabbi: "When a man utters words of the Torah, he never ceases to create spiritual potencies and new lights, which issue like medicines from ever new combinations of the elements and consonants. If therefore he spends the whole day reading just this one verse, he attains eternal beatitude, for at all times, indeed, in every moment, the composition [of the inner linguistic elements] changes in accordance with the condition and rank of this moment, and in accordance with the names that flare up within him at this moment."

The Cabbalist approach to decoding Biblical texts: 1) the outer literal meaning which is considered the first step and not rejected; 2) the allegory; and 3) an inner meaning understood as divine emanations of God into man and man in the role of prophet from God.   Thus the inner meaning becomes a Perpetual Question, and the answer an endlessly changing one depending on the level of being and consciousness of the reader.

Cabbalists avoid descending into extreme relativity by anchoring the true meaning of a sacred text in what they call prophetic intelligence. A 14th century Cabbalist wrote: "It is impossible to comprehend [the inner meaning] of the Torah and the secrets of performing the commandments by "intellectus acquisitus," but by means of the prophetic intellect. ...by the divine intelligence given to the prophets, which is tantamount to the secret of knowledge of the great [divine] name." For Cabbalists decoding can only be done correctly by God-inspired prophets. Metaphors for the emanations of God: levels, powers, sides, areas, worlds, firmaments, pillars, lights, colors, days, gates, streams, garments, crowns.

APPENDIX B Plato on the Limits
to Metaphor and Allegory

Is there a limit to metaphor? Viewed symbolically, let every atom, molecule and organic part of one level of reality (or cosmos) A1 be mapped in a one-to-one ratio into every atom, molecule and part of a higher level B1. Call this mapping reflection and simply represent it as the ratio A1/B1.

Now let the mapping of A1 into B1 be mirrored at higher levels of reality A2, A3, A4, etc., B2, B3, B4, etc.. and let the operator <-->.represent this mirroring process. How a higher level of reality can mirror a lower (and vice versa) need not concern us for now.

To restate our question in terms of mirrors of reflection, is there a limit to A1/B1 <--> A2/B2 <--> A3/B3 <-->...<-->An/Bn, beyond which metaphor collapses into literal-mindedness? If so, that would be the limit to metaphor, there the outer meaning becomes the inner, the inner the outer.

Few in the history of sacred literature have been better qualified to answer this question than Plato. Himself a master of metaphor and allegory, Plato addressed this question in The Republic: "Conceive two levels of reality", he wrote, "One of them the intelligible order, the other the visible...Divide [each level of reality] into two unequal sections." Mathematically, we have two reflections, A1/B1, A2/B2. An outer visible reality consisting of divisions A1, B1, and an inner intelligible order consisting of A2, B2.

"In the visible order", Plato observes, " One division consists of images, that is, shadows, reflections in water and on surfaces, the other division will consist of that of which the first division is an image of: animals, plants, man-made objects..." Symbolically, reflection A1/B1. Plato :"Consider the division of the intelligible...there is one section which the soul is compelled to investigate by treating as images things imitated in [the visible world]" A2 " ...while there is another section... in which [the soul] makes no use of images...relying only on ideas..." B2.

Thinly veiling himself as a student of Euclid, Plato observes: "[Students of geometry] make use of images and talk about them though they are not thinking of them but of those things of which they are a likeness ...The very things which they mold and draw...these things they treat on their turn as only images, but what they really seek is to get sight of those realities which can only be seen by the mind." Again, symbolically, reflection A2/B2. It would seem for Plato the mirroring of reflections stops two levels deep. A1/B1<-->A2/B2.

Why is that?

Plato explains: At the level of visible reality, "compelled to make assumptions, the soul cannot extricate itself from them to reach first principles. Instead it uses images and likenesses to reach a conclusion...But at the level of intelligible reality consisting of ideas only, the soul uses the dialectic to reason through its assumptions, treating them as hypotheses, underpinnings, springboards, not as absolute beginnings, and in this way it rises to the first principle and starting point of all things and after reaching this it proceeds downward to its conclusion without using images or likenesses."

There is no need to go further than two levels, Plato tells us, because by the end of the first reflection A1/B1 it seems one has exhausted the possibilities of metaphor. There is only the literal meaning of the second reflection in the intelligible order A2/B2 based on dialectical reasoning to first principles.

Not so, observed Rumi some 1500 years later. The truth is there are mirrors within mirrors at least six levels deep. In the *Mathnawi* Rumi explains cryptically:

> *Know the words of the Koran are simple,*
> *But within the outward sense is an inner*
> *Secret one. and beneath that secret is a third,*
> *dumbfounding the highest wit.*
> *Seen by none save God, the Incomparable,*
> *the All-Sufficient*
> *Is the fourth meaning, and thus they go on*
> *Even to the seventh meaning.*

Why is that?

Humanity had to wait another 600 years for a plausible resolution. Through the transparency of Gurdjieff's diagram of cosmoses above and below Organic Life one sees 6 cosmoses extending from the invisible intelligible world of the Absolute (World 3), passing down through the visible worlds of Galaxies, Sun, Planets (Worlds 6, 12, and 24) above Organic Life to the imaginary world of the Moon (World 96) below. Each cosmos is a mirror of reflections in the cosmos immediately above and below it.

This mirroring recurs six times. Only four concern us here: The efforts of the steward to escape imagination and be present (Moon) is a metaphor mirroring presence of higher centers (Sun) which in turn mirrors presence of C-Influence (Galaxies), and beyond this, presence of the Absolute transcending metaphor and shattering its mirror. Gurdjieff's solution: The number of levels coincides with the number of cosmoses minus 1 which is six levels (including the shattered mirror for transcendence).

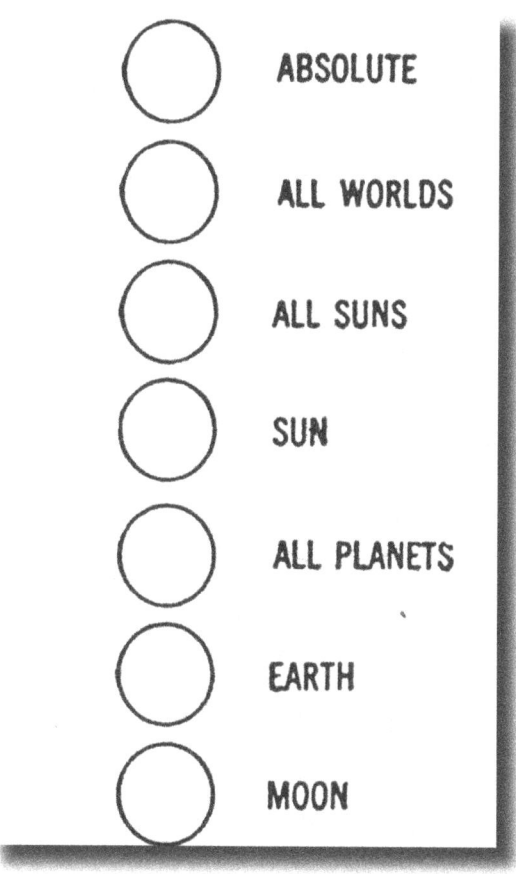

ABSOLUTE

ALL WORLDS

ALL SUNS

SUN

ALL PLANETS

EARTH

MOON

APPENDIX B 2 Keys

Table of Keys: Numbers	
number	meaning
1	Short Be
2	Short Be/Long Be
3	three Be's
4	four wordless breaths
6	a sequence of Work I's
7	sequence of 6 work I's plus Long Be
8	inhaling/exhaling 4 breaths
9	8 plus new sequence
10	sequence of 6 Work I's plus 4 wordless breaths
11	10 plus new Short Be

Table of Keys: States	
state	**psychological meaning**
completing a sequence	6 Work I's repeated in succession silently
Short Be	begin a sequence by dividing attention
Middle Be	bridge the mi-fa interval in a sequence with more efforts to divide attention
Long Be	At the end of a sequence bridge the si-do interval in a sequence by prolonging divided attention with 4 wordless breaths (see below)
3 Be's	Short Be+Middle Be+Long Be
4 wordless breaths	At Long Be in a sequence take in impressions without words or thoughts while breathing in and out 4 times
inhaling 4 wordless breaths	Take in impressions without words or thoughts while breathing in 4 times at Long Be
exhaling 4 breaths	Take in impressions without words or thoughts while breathing out 4 times at Long Be

Table of Keys: Playing Cards	
card	psychological meaning
Joker	higher centers
King of Hearts	intellectual parts of emotional center
Nine of Hearts	emotional part of the intellectual part of emotional center
Queen of Hearts	emotional parts of emotional center
Jack of Hearts	mechanical-moving parts of emotional center
King of Clubs	intellectual parts of instinctive center
Nine of Clubs	emotional part of the intellectual part of instinctive center
Queen of Clubs	emotional parts of instinctive center
Jack of Clubs	mechanical-moving parts of instinctive center

Table of Keys: Colors, Divinities	
colors	**meaning**
blue	presence
red	combustion
divinities	
God	higher centers
god's	Influence C
goddeses	Influence C
angels	Influence C
Horus, Thoth, Osiris	steward
Hathor, Isis	Nine of Hearts
Apopis, Seth, Satan	King of Clubs

Table of Keys:Men, Women, Animals	
men and women	**meaning**
prophets(Moses, Christ, Buddha, Mohammed,etc)	steward
heroes	steward
men	intellectual parts of centers
women	emotional parts of centers
animals, insects	
horses	lower centers
sheep	work I's
goats	mechanical I's
hippotamus	King of Clubs
dung beetle	higher centers
whale	lower centers
worm	King of Clubs
anubis dog	steward
seth dog	King of Clubs
vulture	higher parts of centers
hawk	steward
ibis bird	steward

Table of Keys: Trees, plants, structures, clothing, weapons	

trees, plants, flowers

palm tree	Nine of Hearts
trees, plants, flowers	nine of hearts
burning bush	nine of hearts combusting
lotus	nine of hearts
grapevines	nine of hearts
grass	Work I's
weeds	imagination, mechanical I's
palm leaves	Work I's,
grapes	Work I's

structures, vehicles

doorway, narrow gate	4 wordless breaths
house, man	nine of hearts
temple	
pyramid	a sequence
boat	nine of hearts
carriage	nine of hearts
coffin	Long Be

clothing

garments	Work I's
Red Crown	Short Be combusting
White Crown	Long Be purifying
whip	Work I
rope, staff	sequence
sandals	Work I's

weapons

spear	30 Work I's
arrows	Work I's
sword	Work I's

IMAGE CREDITS

Cover photo: Camel at Sunset, Istock Photos; Floor Mosaic of Hermes Trismegistus, Cathedral of Siena, Italy; John Tenniel, illustration of Humpty Dumpty for Lewis Carroll, Alice in Wonderland; hieroglyphs from W.E.Budge, An Egyptian Hieroglyphic Dictionary; pre-historic cave photos from Jean-Marie Chauvet, Dawn of Art; The Chauvet Cave (Thames & Hudson, 1996); Gurdjieff dance movements: The Initiation of a Priestess. Theatre des Champs-Elysees, 1923; Dervish Prayer: Olgivanna Lloyd Wright, Mme. Galoumian and Jeanne de Salzmann do the 'Camel Step'. Theatre des Champs-Elysees, 1923, Centers of Gravity and Circle of the Many I's, Ouspensky, Psychology of Man's Possible Evolution; Playing Cards

ENDNOTES

1 *Hermes Trismegistus* means "thrice-great Hermes". According to one tradition, in the same way as Christ is considered the Son of God, Hermes Trismegistus was the son of Hermes, a contemporary of Moses (about 1300 BC) directly transmitting his teaching to a line of prophets and philosophers from Zoroaster down to Plato. Another tradition rejects this theory, arguing that unlike Christ, Hermes Trismegistus was not a single individual, but a succession of individuals teaching and writing under that name starting somewhere between 100 AD and 300 AD.

2 As God of mathematics (weights and measures) and writing, Hermes, the Greek messenger God, is a direct descendent of the Egyptian God Thoth, Hermes is also the God of land travel, athletics and thieves.

3 Lao Tzu, Hua Hu Ching, Anonymous Egyptian priests, Book of the Two Ways

4 Why an Egyptian shaman? Graham Hancock's intriguing study (cited below) offers a compelling argument for this being the case.

5 Ibn al-Arabi, Mysteries of Bearing Witness (Great Books of the Islamic World, 2002)

6 Jean Clottes and David Lewis-Williams, Shamans of Prehistory, Graham Hancock, The Supernatural.

7 Quoted in G. Hancock, The Supernatural, p.103.

8 G. Hancock, The Supernatural, pp. 136-142.

9 In Gurdjieff's case, breaking the code of silence may have cost him his connection to Mt. Athos. Ouspenski may very well have parted company with Madame Blatavasky for this reason.

10 G. Gurdjieff, Glimpses, Life is real, only then when I AM, Beelzebub's Tales to His Grandson; P. Ouspenski, In Search of the Miraculous, New Model of The Universe, Psychology of Man's Possible Evolution, The Fourth Way.

11 William P. Patterson, Struggle of the Magicians, p. 91

12   W.P. Patterson, Struggle, p. 92

13   See W.P. Patterson, Struggle. Is this a fairytale to explain and justify Gurdjieff's treatment of Ouspensky? We do not know. Perhaps a mixture of reality and fairytale.

14   W.P. Patterson, Struggle, p.29

15   P.D. Ouspenski, Psychology of Man's Possible Evolution, p. 53.

16   P.D. Ouspenski, Psychology, p. 54

17   W.P. Patterson, Struggle, p.66

18   W.P. Patterson, Struggle, p. 79.

19   W.P. Patterson, Struggle, p. 110

20   W.P. Patterson, Struggle, pp. 177 – 180.

21   At first a student of Ouspenski's, Lord Pendleton became a student of Gurdjieff after Ouspenski's death.

22   P.D. Ouspenski, Psychology, pp.76-77.

23   Ouspenski, Psychology, p.78.

24   See Rodney Collin, Theory of Celestial Influence for a discussion.

25   Ouspenski's Search for the Miraculous was, in fact, a search for keys. Gurdjieff's *Beelzebub's Tales to his*

Grandson is, in fact, Beelzebub's transmission of keys.

26   A student of Alexander Horn, Robert Burton was teaching a version of the Fourth Way for nearly 35 years blending Gurdjieff-Ouspenski ideas with Horn's playing card metaphors. Then in the role of an elderly Rumi, Burton met his Shams in 2005 -- a young Israeli student named Asaf Braverman. The keys were born from the combustion of their friendship.

27   In this instance the phonetic value aaku is supplied by the other hieroglyphs: the crested ibis bird and the sieve.

28   Original full text of Book of Day (based on Alexander Piankoff's translation):

First Hour: "The majesty of this God [Re] comes forth from the Hour whose name is She Who Lifts Up the Beauty of Re. This is the Hour of Appeasement...He appears in the land of the inhabitants of the horizon. Beautiful navigation to make all men, all cattle, all worms, everything he has created live. She rises before Truth."

Second Hour: "The majesty of this God travels in the Hour whose name is She Who Disperses Darkness. This is the Hour of Triumph. It is the Second Hour of the day and the one in which the majesty of this god comes out. His is the Hour of Jubilation and Adoration of Re when he comes out of her. She rises before Will."

-- Text for 3rd, 4th and 5th Hours Missing--

Sixth Hour: "The majesty of this God goes toward the Hour whose name is the Portal Who Seizes. This Hour is the sixth Hour of the day. Rise, rise, let the gods who are in the bark rise in order to repulse Apopis. Let Seth stretch forth his arm to let Apopis fall! – says Isis in her incantation. She rises before Seth."

Seventh Hour: "The voyage of the majesty of this God on the sand bank toward the Hour named She Who Gives Joy, toward this Hour which is the Seventh of the day. The gods in the great bark, their

hearts are joyful after the journey. She rises before Horus."

Eighth Hour: "Passage made by the God over the sand bank toward the Hour called Jubilation. This Hour is the Eighth Hour of the day...the gods who are in [the bark] are in jubilation when Apopis is overthrown and when his majesty is justified. She rises before Khonsu."

Ninth Hour: "This Hour is the Ninth Hour of the day, and the one in which the passage toward the Yaru fields is made while the gods who are in the bark navigate it. She rises before Isis. All the gods come out in great jubilation owing to its greatness, the sky is in beauty, the earth is in peace. These gods take hold of the Nefert-rope, the one which is in the bark. The hearts of the gods in their shrines are in joy, they grant life. Atum, after having passed the sand bank, will overthrow the enemies of Re."

Tenth Hour: "Navigating in peace inside the Tenth Hour, She Who Lights the Sky, who refreshes the oars. It is the Hour to descend in the Bark of the Evening for the crossing in the West. She rises before Magic, the Elder."

Eleventh Hour: "Navigating in peace in the Eleventh

Hour whose name is Beautiful Sight. It is the Hour of adjusting the ropes toward the Western

Horizon when the boat goes down from the West. She rises before He Who Adjusts The Ropes which are in the boat."

Twelfth Hour: "Navigating in peace in the Twelfth Hour whose name is She Who Gives Light in the Island of Life. It is the hour when this God [Re] rests in life in the West and gives offerings, takes care, makes...She rises for the One Who Protects in the twilight."

29   K. Khosla, *The Sufism of Rumi* (Element Books, 1987), p. 21

30   K. Khosla, p. 22

31   K. Khosla, p. 22 – 25

32   K. Khosla, p. 179-180.

33   Source: Clark@Libertypages

34   The 10 emanations are:

Keter Elyon - the highest point above, the crown, the divine Will, the "I am"

Hokhmah - wisdom, hidden thought, primeval being, father, YHWH (upper)

Binah - understanding or intelligence, repentance, palace, mother, Eloheim (upper)

Hesed - love, greatness, goodness, light

Gevurah (din) - power, judgment, fear, wrath, strength, darkness

Tiferet - beauty, mercy, firmanent, YHWH (lower), Sun

Nezah - eternity or endurance

Hod - majesty

Yesod - foundation

Malkhut - kingdom or sovereignty, Israel, supernal earth,

shekhinah (divine presence)

Eloheim (lower), Moon
Source: Clark@Libertypages

35   Rumi, The Masnavi (trrans. E.H. Whinfield, Octagon Press, London, 1979), pg. 169

Book 2: Keys to A Fourth Way School Across Time and Space

CONTENTS

Preface to the Fourth Edition

Preface to The Fourth Edition

i

This fourth edition started out strangely and then grew stranger, and stranger.. One day over breakfast I mentioned casually to two dear friends visiting us from London.to also visit my online bookstore (http://bluelogic.us/). A week later I received an email notice that two of my books had been sold online -- *The Art of Presence*, a printed book by Girard Haven and an ebook by me entitled *Through the Eye of a Needle Part I: Keys Across Time*. At first very pleased by this, I quickly became horrified when the buyer informed she had downloaded the ebook and could not read it. Downloading a copy myself, I experienced a Nightmare on Elms Street moment. The ebook text looked like it had just gone through a shredding machine.

Who was the intrepid buyer?

None other than one of my dear friend from London.

I quickly replaced the Shredding Machine Copy with a fresh unshredded ebook and sent it to her over the Internet only to discover that Part II had never been uploaded to the server. No Part II? Three years had passed without me posting it. Only Part I went up, and that one shredded to bits without me knowing it.

Reading the manuscript for Part II, I thanked Providence I failed to upload it to the server. I could not believe I was the same person who wrote it. Quickly I realized I wasn't. The author who wrote Part II three years ago is not the general editor writing this Preface today. Rightly or wrongly, for good or bad, I see things quite differently now. Maybe not so differently as night from day, but almost. More like night (then) from twilight (now). I had simply outgrown Part II and the author who wrote it -- precisely because of the author who wrote and believed in it.

So why am I publishing Part II now if I am such a New Man?

ii

Three years ago I was still under the hypnotic spell of a discovery that turned my previous way of thinking upside down (or right side up depending on your frame of reference): To me I had discovered St. Peter's Keys: a system of keys and symbols for not just unlocking the mystery of hermetic thinking. That had been tried and done before. No, Robert Earl Burton had found a way to do this consistently for ALL the ancient teachings. Not just the Bible (new & Old) and Koran, but all of them -- Buddhist texts, Hindu, St. Augustine, Philokalia, Lao Tzu. Here it was: a Rosetta Stone decoding what would otherwise still be incomprehensible nonsense to us. No one else had done this before or, if they had, few were talking. Only this controversial man -- Robert Earl Burton -- had discovered a Rosetta Stone for decoding the hermetic teachings -- one might say his own Rosetta Stone, but it worked -- and he was not just talking about it but using it to teach with.

Had I gone insane?

Read Part II and judge for yourself.

Applying Burton's keys first to The Amduat and then to The Old and New Testaments I quickly discovered what was going on: Interchangeability of outer meanings for the same inner meaning-- the Rosetta Stone effect. The discovery was intoxicating.

In *Out of Africa: The Amduat* I wrote: [1]

"1) The Egyptian hieroglyphs for "God" and "Lord" not only have a literal meaning far removed from our Judeo-Christian conception, but an inner psychological meaning recognizable to any student of one of the great hermetic traditions -- Buddhist, Sufi, Taoist, Platonic, Cabalist, Gnostic, Philokalia, Fourth Way. Within the local frame of reference of any one hermetic tradition the decoding principle is both simple and unifying:[2]

A) Map the highest religious entity and level of being into our highest state of inner psychological existence (the Sun God Ra, Yahweh, Vishnu, the Tao, etc. mapped into higher centers, presence, World 6 and 12).

B) Map intermediate entities into the psychological attitudes and practices required to reach the highest state (Yin-Yang, Osiris, Horus, Isis, Brahma, the Wise Pharaoh, Solomon, Moses, Plato, Christ, Mary Magdalena, Buddha, Mohammed, Lao Tzu, Tarot Card 21 mapped into a fine-

---

1   G. Moore, Out of Africa: The Amduat (Blue Logic, 2010)
2   First strange paradox: Since each tradition has an intimate connection to a world religion of one kind or another, why the strange tension and disconnect at some point between the two? Why this apparent parting of the ways over time between practices based on the literal meaning and those based on their inner psychological truth.

grained emotional intelligence able to separate wheat from chaff, into an inner psychological steward using this intelligence, and the practice causing the separation and called by many names: mantra, Jesus prayer, Platonic recollection, self-remembering, sequencing.

C) Map the lowest religious entity into the psychological states resisting those practices (Apopis, Seth, Satan, etc. mapped into the elusive intelligence of the instinctive center able to resist by seeming to agree and able not to agree by seeming not to resist; except when hidden and unseen, always seeming, and never simply being.) [3]"

"The inherent logic behind this mapping process enforces invariance across time, space, religions and traditions: the inner meaning of metaphors and symbols from one tradition are interchangeable with those from the others -- without exception. This does not mean, however, they are the same (although they can be for all we know, which we don't know), just interchangeable.

4. Applied consistently to sacred Egyptian texts Burton's system of keys reveals a strange psychological universe

---

[3]   Second paradox: Do these mapping algorithms mean the religious entities (Ra, Yahweh, God, Vishnu, Osiris, Isis, Apopis, Seth and Satan) and the historical teachers (Buddha, Plato, Mohammed, Jesus, Solomon) cannot be taken literally apart from the inner meaning of their teachings? Yes. Then does that mean they have no independent existence apart from whatever inner psychological truth they reveal to us? Yes. So does that
mean then that at the highest level God is Presence, and Presence is God? Yes.

of higher and lower centers entering and exiting, of states ranging from imagination to the 4th state of presence, and perpetual warfare between the highest and lowest parts of the biological machine. In the specific case of The Amduat, this universe has a simple, but no less miraculous, story to tell: Between successive moments of presence higher centers must descend into the 2nd state to the very edge of imagination, gradually losing presence in a running battle with the instinctive center until they die, and there in death presence is re-ignited mysteriously. On a metaphorical 24-hour cycle, the descent to this level takes roughly 6 hours, followed by 6 hours of ascent to the dawn of the 4th state. On the scale of a prayer sequence in real time, it can happen in more or less sixty seconds."

"5. The message of The Amduat is clearer: To return to their highest level of existence, to regain the inner Paradise Lost, our higher emotional and higher intellectual centers must somehow first die to the lowest level. This rebirth-in-death is represented in the image of "Body of Ra" (the steward) fusing with Khepri (higher centers) at midnight in complete darkness, the light of Ra (presence) having been completely extinguished. In that moment rebirth-in-death is the mystery of a man-beetle stretched out head-to-toe igniting the spark of new life inside the protective coil of a serpent swallowing its tail.

6. How, practically speaking, do higher centers die to be reborn? This is the central mystery, the "hidden chamber" beyond analysis and words.[4]

There is no "practical" answer. The Amduat tells us only

---

4   The original Egyptian title for The Amduat is "Treatise from the Hidden Chamber."

this much: Speaking thru the head of Osiris, in the 6th hour, Ra says: "O Radiant One guarding My Image! O Purification of the Gods!... May My Image Remain hidden! May this darkness become Light, And breath enter the members of My Flesh. Guard me while I pass by you in peace." True, the declamation "may this darkness become light" refers to the second state of consciousness being transformed into presence. And "[May] breath enter the members of My Flesh" seems an explicit, almost literal reference to the steward ("My Flesh") in the act of inhaling the higher state of presence. But the passage's main point is pointing in another direction: "May My Image Remain hidden!" No words, no images, a mystery transcending logical explanation."

iii

Six years later the author of the above remarkable passage has outgrown its naive statement of a vision -- Robert Burton's vision of the invariance of inner meanings from one hermetic school to another. At the same time, he has confirmed its validity.

How is this paradox possible?

Answer: One does not have to interchange every system of hermetic keys with every other to confirm that, with few exceptions, they are usually interchangeable. It is about probabilities and likelihoods of being interchangeble, not about absolute certainties. Even if one faced an infinite series of keys and symbols and an infinite Sisyphus process of selecting and comparing one set of keys to another, one could safely predict that the most likely outcome in most instances will be a congruence of keys, a confirmation of the same inner meaning more or less. And that is because the mathematics of mapping, and specifically of mapping ordered sets into one another enforces this outcome most of the time.

iv

The above revelation came to me at the 11th Hour of writing this preface. Down to the wire, a photo finish: Only minutes before that I wrote and then erased: "So why publish this second volume?. For its historical value?" And then I added this prophetic line: "It is usually unwise to reject the past simply because one has outgrown it. Especially ones own past. One simply embraces it without believing in it so naively anymore. One accepts it on new terms." Forget historical value. Old terms, new terms, same terms. We confirm invariance most of the time. Did naively assuming this work six years ago? Yes, it worked then. Does it work now? Let readers be the judge.

G. Moore
2016

I. Sequences: A Ladder to Paradise...

The ladder leading to the Kingdom [of God] is concealed within you, that is, in your soul. Wash yourself from sin, and you will see the rungs of the ladder by which you can ascend.

Philokalia

I

Recurrence at the Gates of Hell. Racing ahead, humanity is always arriving back to the same crossroad -- a crossroad with strangely recurring spacetime coordinates: always arriving back it seems just before sunset. Compare the opening scene of The Amduat nearly 3,600 years ago: At twilight in the evening, before descending into the Netherworld, Ra is greeted by Seth. In Dante's Divine Comedy some ninteen hundred years later: Again at twilight, Dante's path is barred by a menacing Lion, and in CS Lewis, The Great Divorce of Heaven and Hell published 650 years later during a twilight that never darkens to a night that never comes the Narrator is confronted by the same bully at the same bus stop.

What if the same crossroad is here again, but this time on this page you are reading? Spooky, yes? Quite literally: What if continuing straight ahead down this smooth and easy time path of literal-minded thinking, you read a few paragraphs or words further before dozing off or throwing the book in the trash and sinking slowly into the comforting mud and quicksand of your imaginary picture of one-self: --"I've got better things to be doing than this" --, in the swamp of one identification after another with your biological existence (money, sex, food, material comfort or discomfort, petty dangers and pleasures of the moment) -"She was cute...How am I going to pay the rent..." "put the reset button at q-square minus pi over 2..". -- and one's imaginings about others and what they think or don't think of you - "Did I say the right thing"..."did he notice my new hairstyle...", and about ones world, what's happening or not happening in it -"Jesus, I'm getting scared, when is this global recession going to end..." A chaos of I's always gyrating and swirling around the same paradoxical gravity point: Non-existent nothingness existing nonetheless -- in ones mind.

Barred by the one-way arrow of time, one cannot turn around and retreat back up the path of literal-mindedness to the safety of past states nor turn left or right to escape since there is no left or right. Time is one dimensional -- at least as we experience it. No up or down either. Only forward or backward. And going backward is prohibited by entropy, the second law of thermodynamics. What then? Only forward and either recur or not recur.

The Inferno. Over the Gates of Hell in Dante's *Divine Comedy* there is an inscription. Usually only its last sentence is quoted: " Abandon Hope all ye who enter here." The complete inscription is even more revealing, however. It reads:

> Through Me lies the road to the City of Grief,
> Through Me lies the path to suffering eternal,Through Me lies the road to lost souls,
> Justice compelled my Mighty Architect,
> the Power Divine, to construct Me,
> Before I existed, nothing was save the Eternal.
> I shall exist forever. Abandon Hope all ye who enter here. [5]

This is an epitaph for all of us destined to recur. We are continuing down the path of sleep and becoming trapped here in the Me, Me, Me of our Many I's. This is our biological existence as we live it mechanically every second of every hour of every day – even though the opportunity not to do so disappears and then re-appears all the time. [6]

5   Dante Alighieri, *The Divine Comedy* (trans. L.G. White)
6   Read Peter Ouspensky, *The Strange Life of Ivan Osakin:* Ivan has memory of future events but he cannot use this foreknowledge to avoid repeating the events of his life because every time he is about to do something different to avoid recurring, he falls asleep and wakes up again only after the recurring event has already happened.

Considering the stakes, what does going forward in time to not recur mean? Stripped of its metaphorical clothing, it means that one must learn how to interrupt ones negative fears and imaginings, but also ones positive expectations, and stop day-dreaming about these. But how can one stop doing what one is not even aware one is doing?

Short answer: One cannot stop without outside help.

II

Psychologically, it's always Groundhog's Day just outside the Gates of Hell, and at first we have to only register this, become aware of it. Becoming aware slowly gives one the strength to stop going forward and descending psychologically. Then one has to have the courage and will to make efforts to ascend the bumpy, mentally challenging but emotionally rewarding path of psychological thinking, very small efforts at first. A part of these small efforts involve retrieving and actually reading sacred texts written for this purpose from different ancient traditions (Buddhist, Judeo-Christian, Moslem, etc) and not just one's pet favorite. The efforts grow a little to helping others when one can, to silent and intentional efforts to be present, at first with difficulty and then more easily, but never without effort. Descending is easy and requires almost zero effort. But this ascending business at the Gates of Hell is definitely an oddity of Creation. Why just there? In the Inferno it's impossible. In Paradise unnecessary. Where else then for maximum practical effect.

The meaning: Ascending has been called many things: repentance (which literally means "a turning"), atonement, acts of kindness, small or large, a smile, a few words of encouragement, a helping hand, without expectation of re-payment, etc. Its two main properties though are continual recurrence just on the verge of entering imagination (its Eternal Groundhog Day property) and the presence of mind intrinsic to it of literally and simply being present to whatever is in front of one. That means we are talking about stopping recurrence on the scale of seconds.

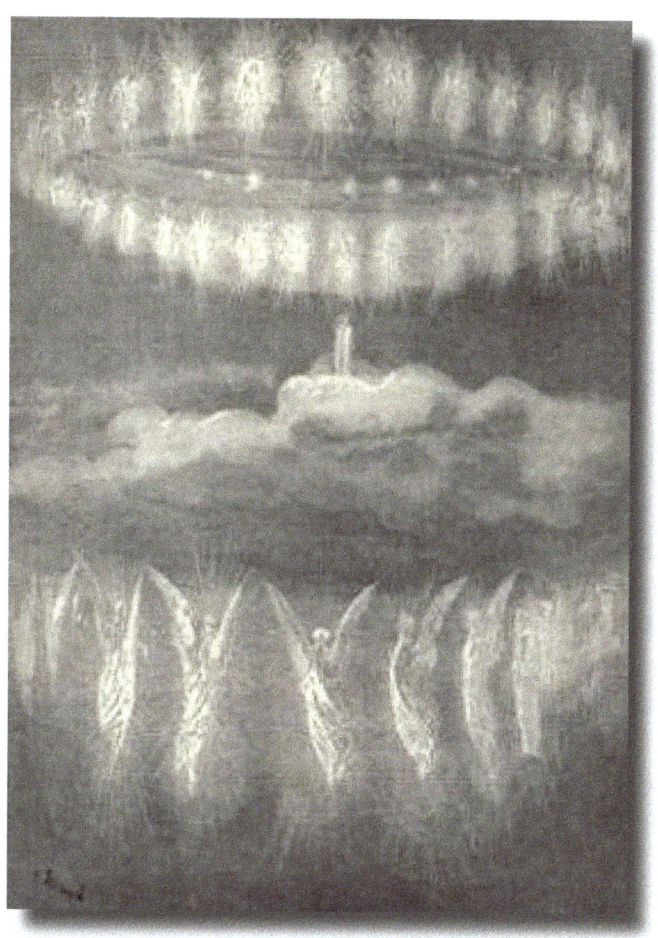

Why is it better to go up this time path with efforts to be present rather than down it in effortless sleep? What purpose does this serve? Gurdjieff talks about doing this to reduce the suffering of the Absolute.[7] Sufi Masters were insistent on humanity using every breath for one thing: the continuous remembrance of God (zikr).[8] The Desert

---

7   G. Gurdjieff, Beelzebub's Tales to His Grandson
8   K. Khosla, The Sufism of Rumi

Fathers of the Gnostic Nag Hammadi and Philokalia were equally emphatic: insisting on continual repetition of the Jesus prayer to fill ones heart and mind with the memory of God.

III

In this essay readers will be introduced to a new addition to those great hermetic traditions: the six-syllable sequence.[9] The form has changed, the ancient purpose has not, the bottle is new, the wine is not, it's still the same and quite intoxicating. Grown, harvested and fermented to ignite in the soul a flame of desire for continuous self-remembrance. Is this not more enjoyable than sleep? For what after all is sleep? A continual forgetting and falling away from zikr, from the remembrance of God, a continual descending into Hell, the chaotic Inferno of our many I's.

Sequencing the Law of Seven. For those of us brought up in the West, the following succession of eight musical notes should sound familiar (pun intended): C,D,E,F,G, A,B,C. Our ears grew up with it. It is called a twelve-tone musical scale or octave (octave meaning "eight", twelve tones because in addition to the eight natural tones, there are four sharps and four flats).

Musical octaves have some interesting properties. Imagine a well-tempered piano of infinite length. If one plays the eight notes in succession (no flats or sharps) and ascends to higher levels, playing from left to right, the notes will recur. For example, the first note C will recur at higher and higher frequencies, the note D will recur, and so will E,F,G and so on until the sound passes out of our audible frequency range. Secondly, between the 3rd and 4th notes (E and F)

9   Robert E. Burton, Weekly Notes (unpublished papers)

there is a musical interval called the mi-fa interval; and between the 7th and 8th notes (B and C) there is another interval called the si-do interval.

At these two intervals the pitch frequencies slow down. In music this happens no matter what instrument one plays or at what frequency. Starting at C, the energy passing through the octave dampens at the 3rd note and again at the 7th. No one knows why. It just does. It is one of many properties in physics that has no explanation (entanglement is another).

Gurdjieff was the first to apply this extraordinary property to everything that exists, calling it the Law of Seven. Everything that exists, he explained, is either ascending or descending because of it. In this context, he attached special practical significance to intervals. Everything ascending, without exception, has to first pass through a mi-fa interval and then, if it bridges the interval, through a si-do interval. Without exception, all the time.

And what happens if one does not "bridge the interval"? Wrong question. Intervals must be bridged, one way or another. This is a law. The real practical question is, will one bridge it ascending to a higher level or state of consciousness, or bridge it descending to a lower state? If one bridges it descending, that means ascent has somehow been broken off, and one has entered a new, descending octave, passing quickly thru a si-do interval, usually without noticing it, and then descending slowly like Alice inside the rabbit hole to the mi-fa, only to drop abruptly into the do of a new, lower octave. How then does one not get stuck there? How does one begin to re-ascend?. These questions suggest a good working definition of Hell: Getting stuck in Me, Me, Me and not desiring to ascend anymore.

To bridge the interval ascending at si-do or mi-fa one simply has to bring more energy to the interval than exists there mechanically. Gurdjieff suggested ways to do this -- without spelling out a recipe.[10] This might sound clinical and antiseptic. But clinical sounding or not, one has to make more efforts than one would otherwise make ordinarily. Otherwise one remains trapped. What kind of efforts? Intelligent efforts for the specific purpose of turning to the right and ascending. That's what Work I's are. Simple (and difficult) as that. Gurdjieff and Ouspensky called these intelligent efforts conscious shocks. There are two kinds they taught us: The shock generated by self-remembering and the shock released by connecting momentarily (or permanently) with C Influence. In fact, that is what "bridging the interval" means practically: Making more efforts intelligently to ascend. Otherwise one descends.[11]

Sequencing in theory. Sequences represent a special category of ascending octaves – special because they are one of the few octaves that connect the soul consistently with higher centers, at first briefly, but then for longer periods of time, and finally permanently. In the Philokalia tradition the Desert Fathers call them simply, and less clinically, Jesus prayers.[12]

Even though sequences have only six steps, they have all the properties of an 8-note ascending octave: recurrence of steps, movement to higher levels, intervals, the break-

10   G. Gurdjieff, Life is Real Only Then When I am
11   P. Ouspensky, In Search of the Miraculous

12 Anonymous Russian Monk, Way of A Pilgrim. The original prayer: "Lord Jesus Christ, have mercy on me". In six syllables it is simply: "Lord, have mercy on me."

ing of ascent at the intervals if not enough intelligent effort is made. This is because, in reality, a 6-step sequence is an 8-note octave. How is that possible? Look at an octave and a sequence side-by-side:[13]

A Musical Octave	A Sequence
C (DO)	1 – Short Be
D (RE)	2 – Hold
E (MI)	3– Work I
---} interval	--- } interval
F (FA)	4–Middle Be
G (SO)	5– Work I
A (LA)	6 – Long BE
B (SI)	
--- } interval	
C (DO)	

13 There are interesting parallels between DNA sequencing and sequencing Work I's. For example, the method of simplifying observations and primarily looking for and writing out the succession of nucleotide subunits (adenine (A), cytosine(C), guanine (G), thymine (T)) is called DNA sequencing, and the observed succession, for example, AAAGTCTGAC is a DNA sequence. By observing the mechanical I of the moment, selecting a Work I to displace it as the theme and then "writing out" (i.e., going through) a succession of 6 Work I's to divide attention -- with the theme at the 3rd and 5th Step -- we are, in effect, simplifying self-remembering to sequencing Work I's, six at a time.

Until the 6th step octaves and sequences are identical. But at the 6th step something remarkable happens: The sequence stretches to include the last three notes of the octave – A, B, C or LA, SI, DO – plus the si-do interval. That is why it is called Long BE: it covers a distance at least three times as long as the first step (called Short Be being roughly a third the duration of Long BE) and on top of that it includes an interval. The si-do interval hidden inside the 6th step is the reason this step is such a hazardous achievement.

In Hour 3 of The Amduat Ancient Egyptians humorously called the 6th Step "Boat That Capsizes", and we see why: Horus (the soul) happens to be balancing himself precariously on a serpent (the lower self).

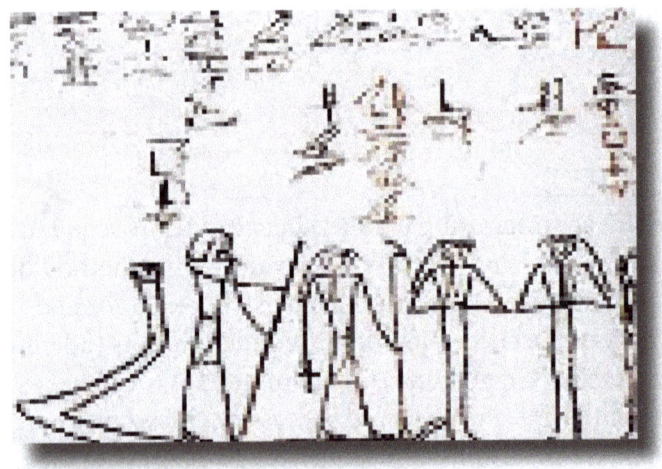

Sequencing in practice. In hieroglyphic texts in Ancient Egypt we come across the hieroglyph heka, meaning literally "a work of magic" and translated "spell or incantation". "A work of magic" is an ancient key for a Work I. Why magic? We are made up of literally thousands of mechanical I's (by one estimate about 10,000 each day) coming in, and going out of, existence all the time, sometimes ascending to high states for a moment, then descending and sometimes plummeting abruptly to a psychological low. A chaotic Inferno of I's.

Over and against this, we have a pathetically small band of Work I's, and must consider ourselves eternally lucky to have those. By one estimate, there are altogether less than a hundred Work I's and, practically speaking, no more than thirty actively used for everyday purpose. 10,000 mechanical Is to 100 Work Is equals 100-to-one odds of remaining trapped forever inside the Inferno of our chaotic mechanical I's. Therefore nothing less than heka or magic is needed to escape.

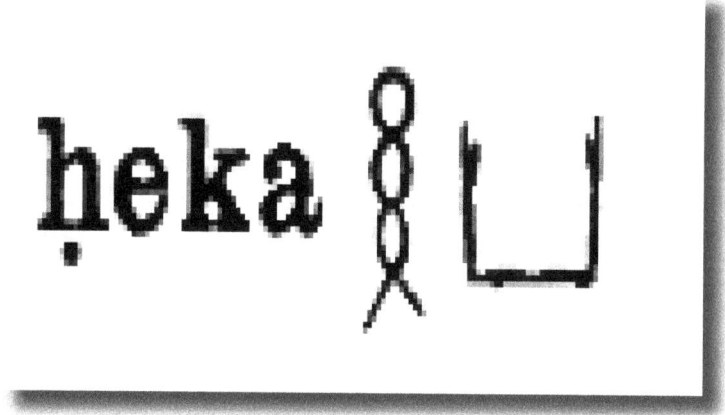

Heka is the miracle of David with a slingshot facing off Goliath, of Christ dividing a loaf of bread into 5,000 loaves, and transforming water into wine. One Work I says simply "Be", a one- syllable word meaning literally: "pierce the veil of imagination, be present". Another one-syllable Work I says "Gods" and instructs the soul to "remember the Gods, another says Drop, and your account against some is cancelled (momentarily). Heka, work of magic, our soul ascends.

Let's back up a little: What's a mechanical I, and what's a Work I?

Mechanical I's. The basic unit of perception for any movement, sensation, emotion or thought is called an I. An I can be a slow-moving thought, "1 + 1 = 2", a faster-moving gesture of the arms "Turning right!" – or an even faster moving sensation, say, of pain, "Ouch!" Even faster than this is the speed of emotional perceptions, "What a beautiful rose." Perceptions relating to sex are even faster: Split-second choice of mate, smells, etc. Long before the intellectual brain is aware of what has happened, the sex center has registered and acted on the I, "She's pretty."

Far from being unified and just one big ego, we are, in fact, a strange stream of many tiny I's being born and perishing every few seconds: "1 + 1 = 2", "Turning right!", "Ouch!", "What a beautiful rose!", "She's pretty." Over the course of 24 hours, we are thousands of I's. One estimate places the number at about 10,000 a day; and it calls them the 10,000 mechanical I's. If true, that would mean that most of the time we are about 10 mechanical I's coming and going every minute, or about one I every 6 seconds.

Work I's - Rungs of A Ladder to Paradise. Subject to the same laws of mechanicality -- enduring usually for only seconds -- Work I's are nonetheless not mechanical, they do not come and go in random 6-second bursts over the course of a day. Work I's are literally the product of intentional efforts to be present and escape. Appearing singularly as our own private efforts to not express negative emotions, to avoid greed, to not self-deprecate, etc. and culminating in brief moments of presence, Work I's are small quantum packets of will literally akin to photons of light: Serve, Kneel, Child, Drop, Be, Serve, etc.

Over time these packets form rungs on a ladder for eventually reaching a permanent state of presence. Not at first but eventually. At first, we rise on them a step or two for a moment and then fall back down just as far (or farther). Going to their root property, however, on this Jacob's Ladder Work I's are all of the above -- non-mechanical, products of effort, packets of will resembling photons of light -- but they are something more as well: Above all else they confirm the existence of an esoteric School, being its main by-product. Put bluntly, unlike mechanical Is, without schools, Work I's would not exist. Not even the cleverest magician could invent them.

The Special School Function of Work I's. Work I's are used to teach the soul how to ascend the ladder of being, consciousness and will. Like John the Baptist they point to the Christ within each one of us without being the Anointed One themselves. Each Work I is, in effect, a little John the Baptist with a smile and a finger pointing up to something greater than it. At St. Catherine's monastery there is a painting which vividly captures the psychological meaning of all of this. The painting depicts monks ascending a ladder despite the fierce opposition of demons trying to pull them off. The ladder extends from the Gates of Hell to Paradise -- from the Inferno of our chaotic mechanical I's to the Paradise of a simple wordless presence beyond the I's.

monastery there is a painting which vividly captures the chaotic mechanical I's to the Paradise of a simple worless-presence beyond the I's.

The monks represent the active first force of the soul using one sequence after another of to push off each Work I, ascend and reach this state. The demons are mechanical I's trying to disrupt the effort. Sometimes they succeed, a sequence is broken, and the soul tumbles back into the Inferno of chaotic I's. The ladder itself represents part of the third force, the human element, and consists of sequences of Work Is, each rung being a Work I. This third force also has a transcendent element, however, consisting of our aim to be present psychologically. Easily confused with everyday aims, this aim is quite different, representing the internal impulse our soul receives directly from higher centers (the God within) at the quantum electronic level.[14]

Storming Paradise Without A School. Can one use sequences by oneself without the help of an esoteric school? Since nothing is forbidden, anything is possible. One can try. Just remember though: the Ladder to Paradise is a ladder of Work I's, and these I's belong to a specific school at a specific

14 In the Fourth Lecture of his Psychology of Man's Possible Evolution, Ouspensky presented a schematic box diagram of a man standing sideways to illustrate the principle of the sixfold division of the soul. He called each division a center of gravity or simply a center, one center for intellectual activity, a second for moving or motor-sensory activity, a third for instinctive and a fourth for emotional perceptions. Collectively, he called these the four lower centers and did so to sharply differentiate them from a pair of activities he called higher emotional and higher intellectual centers or simply higher centers. (not shown on the diagram) These higher centers are the seat of revelations, mystical dreams, even mathematical and scientific discoveries. Without proof, since there is none, Ouspensky argued that while all six centers are housed in the machine and depend on it for their existence, the pair of higher centers could survive the shock of death and even pass on to another lifetime, the four lower centers could not. He called this ability consciousness without functions. On the scale of a machine its higher centers are immortal, literally Gods within us.

time, meaning they usually come with special instructions (to avoid injury, explosions, etc) not written down anywhere. Suppose, however, some mercurial Prometheus of the 4th Way steals a ladder or two, distributing free copies of them for himself and friends to use outside their school of origin. What then? Again one can try. Mouravieff and other Eastern orthodox monks claim that Gurdjieff did just that: Stole their keys to Paradise and stormed it with the help of Ouspensky, Orage and others.[15]

That may or may not be true. Point is, it really doesn't matter. In a universe where nothing is forbidden and anything is possible, at the end of the day the only real practical question is, did they succeed in storming it? Outside the orthodox monastery Mouravieff belonged to the general consensus is they did. This only demonstrates that 100-to-1 odds against succeeding without the outside help of a School are still just that – only odds -- not a law of the universe. In our post-heretic-burning era private ladder-climbing remains a valid option.

---

15   Boris Mouravieff, Gnosis, (1989) vols 1-3.

II. ...and four wordless breaths

God's speech is without letters, no sound, no voice.
Najm al-Din Razi

Keys: their literal meaning. Literally, a key is an instrument made of metal for locking and unlocking a door to a house or room or opening a container or starting the engine of a car. Locking itself is the act of preventing access into or out of the room or container. In everyday life, the reasons for locking may range from simply wanting to maintain privacy to preventing theft of one's car, valuable trade secrets or sensitive military documents. In the case of sacred texts, most have been written in such a way that their literal meaning becomes both a lock concealing knowledge of the inner meaning and a key for disclosing it.

Genesis. Take this passage from Genesis: "In the beginning God created the heaven and the earth. And the earth was without form, and void; and darkness was upon the face of the deep. And the Spirit of God moved upon the face of the waters. And God said, Let there be light: and there was light. And God saw the light, that it was good."

Taken literally, the passage is describing the creation of the world. That is the outer meaning known to humanity generally for thousands of years. What is the inner meaning? Is there any? In "Keys: Metaphors Across Time for the War Within" above we discussed the choices. EITHER there is and the systems of Gurdjieff, Ouspensky, Collin, Horn and Burton are simply maps for finding this inner meaning. OR there isn't -- either because there never was an inner meaning or it has been lost.

The inner meaning. Assuming Genesis has an inner meaning, how does one gain access to it? In the passage taken from Genesis, besides their literal meaning, Burton sees in the words "beginning", "God", "heaven" "earth" "darkness", "water" and "light" keys with a non-literal meaning. For example, Burton considers "in the beginning" a key for piercing the veil of imagination with the word Be, "God" is a key for higher centers, "heaven" is a key for presence, "earth" for the nine of hearts*, "darkness" for the 2nd state, "water" for imagination, and "light" for the 3rd state. (*See Glossary)

Using the above keys, the inner meaning can be unlocked: "Piercing the veil of imagination with Be, higher centers create both presence and the nine of hearts -- but a nine of hearts still in the 2nd state, and presence just on the edge of that state ("the Spirit of God upon the face of the waters"). From there higher centers create the 3rd state, and observe their own presence".

Thanks to keying, one sees that the first lines of Genesis are describing a fundamental psychological event: higher centers producing a presence in us beyond our 2nd state experience – a presence we point to with the words "four wordless breaths"-- which is beyond those words. [16]

The first sequence. Look carefully at the opening lines of Genesis: "In the beginning God created the heaven and the earth. And the earth was without form, and void; and

16   How do we know these keys -- or any keys for that matter -- are true? Short answer: Starting out, we don't know. We can only confirm their truth over time by using them. Keys are metaphors confirmed or falsified in our practical work over time.

darkness was upon the face of the deep. And the Spirit of God moved upon the face of the waters. And God said, Let there be light: and there was light. And God saw the light, that it was good."

The text is not simply about sequences, it is itself a sequence, but a special sequence, it is literally the sequence during the split second presence (heaven) and the Nine of Hearts (earth) come into existence at Short Be. ONE: "In the beginning God created the heaven and the earth." TWO: "And the earth was without form, and void;" signifying the emptiness of a receptive emotional center. THREE: "and darkness (imagination) was upon the face of the deep (the lower centers)." FOUR: "And the Spirit of God (presence of higher centers) moved upon the face of the waters. (across the surface of imagination)" FIVE: "And God (higher centers) said, Let there be light (presence): and there was light." SIX: "And God saw the light, that it was good."

More Genesis. "8. And the Lord God planted a garden in Eden; and there He put the man he had formed. And out of the ground the Lord God made to grow every tree that is pleasant to sight and good for food, the tree of life also in the midst of the garden, and the tree of the knowledge of good and evil. 18. Then the Lord God said: 'It is not good that man should be alone...' "so out of the ground the Lord God formed every beast of the field and every bird of the air, and brought them to man to see what he would call them; and whatever the man called every living creature, that was its name. The man gave names to all cattle and to the birds of the air, and to every beast of the field..."

More hidden messages. Adding several more keys: "garden" for man's inner psychological state, "good" for being present, "man" for steward, "ground" for nine of

hearts, "every tree that is pleasant, etc" for mechanical I's, "tree of life" for the four wordless breaths evoking eternal presence, "tree of the knowledge of good and evil" for the sequence invoked by knowing the difference between presence ("good") and imagination ("evil") and "names" for keys.

Using the keys, we unearth the following: Higher centers populate the inner psychological state of the steward with mechanical I's of every kind, with Work I's in general and with Work I's dealing specifically with the steward's mortality and self-remembering. Higher centers send the steward I's of every kind -- mechanical and non-mechanical -- for keying. In this ground state the steward is still in the 3rd state (the state of higher emotions), and being there, it does not know the difference between presence and imagination.

The Garden of Eden represents our original psychological state -- a state of presence before the steward enters imagination and "knows" the difference. How does the steward learn the difference?

135

Falling before the Fall: Genesis prepares us for a shocking answer. ". The man gave names to all cattle and to the birds of the air, and to every beast of the field; but for the man there was not found a helper fit for him. So the Lord God caused a deep sleep to fall upon the man."

"Deep sleep" is a key for being deep in the 2nd state, so deep, in fact, that one is on the verge of slipping into 1st state. Genesis is describing a fall before the Fall. Higher centers are making the steward descend from the 3rd state of keying with presence to an abysmally low second state on the edge of 1st state -- a dream state while in the waking state, a virtual reality called imagination. There the Nine of Hearts is re-created a 2nd time by higher centers, but this time as "woman" instead of "Earth": "While [man] slept [God] took one of his ribs and closed up its place with flesh, and the rib...He made into a woman and brought her to the man."

Waking up, the steward returns to keying with presence. "This is at last bone of my bone," he says, "And flesh of my flesh; she shall be called Woman, because she was taken out of man." With "woman" for Nine of Hearts, "bone" for the intellectual parts of centers and "flesh" for a sequence, the steward is now keying himself, he is one and the same as the Nine of Hearts completing a sequence, an intellectual part born from an intellectual part, one sequence born from another.

John Milton on Eve's Dream. In Book 5 of Paradise Lost John Milton gives us a different view. According to Milton, it is the Nine of Hearts itself, not the steward, which descends into the 2nd state and fails to remember itself. Milton writes:

Now Morn her rosie steps in th' Eastern Clime

Advancing, sow'd the Earth with Orient Pearle,
When ADAM wak't, so customd, for his sleep
Was Aerie light, from pure digestion bred,
And temperat vapors bland, which th' only sound
Of leaves and fuming rills, AURORA's fan,
Lightly dispers'd, and the shrill Matin Song
Of Birds on every bough; so much the more
His wonder was to find unwak'nd EVE
/With Tresses discompos'd, and glowing Cheek,
/As through unquiet rest:

ADAM is a key for the steward remembering himself
mechanically, but not so EVE. She is not simply a key for
the Nine of Hearts in the 2nd state. She has become the
Nine of Hearts experiencing a state within the 2nd state
never experienced before, a sleep within sleep. Adam
"finds unwak'nd EVE/With Tresses discompos'd, and
glowing Cheek,/ As through unquiet rest" Unable to return
to presence mechanically, EVE dreaming is a key for being
in imagination with zero effort to be present.. But why the
unquiet rest"? Milton writes:

O Sole in whom my thoughts find all repose,
My Glorie, my Perfection, glad I see
Thy face, and Morn return'd, for I this Night,
Such night till this I never pass'd, have dream'd,
If dream'd, not as I oft am wont, of thee,
Works of day pass't, or morrows next designe,
But of offence and trouble, which my mind
Knew never till this irksom night.

What was Eve's offence? What disturbed her so? Milton describes the dream: Satan is eating the forbidden fruit, and then suddenly he turns to Eve:

Here, happie Creature, fair Angelic EVE,
Partake thou also; happie though thou art,
Happier thou mayst be, worthier canst not be:
Taste this, and be henceforth among the Gods
But somtimes in the Air, as wee, somtimes
Ascend to Heav'n, by merit thine, and see
What life the Gods live there, and such live thou.
So saying, he drew nigh, and to me held,
Even to my mouth of that same fruit held part
Which he had pluckt; the pleasant savourie smell
So quick'nd appetite, that I, methought,
Could not but taste.

Eve is deeply disturbed because she has given permission to Satan to tempt her without offering any resistance whatsoever. How could she since ADAM, the steward, is her only resistance? Without his presence, the dream foreshadows, the King of Clubs will draw a willing Nine of Hearts into imagination. Eve remembers this and is saddened. Adam tries to console her. "She was cheered," Milton writes, "But silently a gentle tear let fall From either eye, and wip'd them with her haire."

The Fall Itself. The steward and Nine of Heart's are fated to discover the difference between presence and imagination. Both being intellectual parts of the emotional center, it is bound to happen sooner or later. But how? Not from the emotional center. No, their discovery requires outside help -- in this case from an intellectual part of our biological machine every bit as intelligent as the steward and Nine of Hearts.

Genesis tells us: "3.1. Now the serpent was more subtle [i.e., clever] than any other wild creature the Lord had made." "Serpent" is a key for the intellectual part of the instinctive center, the King of Clubs. Gifted with intelligence, the King of Clubs is lacking just one thing: an emotional connection to higher centers. Lacking this, it is the perfect tempter. "3.4. You will not die [if you eat fruit from the tree of knowledge]", it tells the woman. "For God knows that when you eat of it your eyes will be opened, and you will be like God, knowing good and evil".

The Fall begins in this moment, in the temptation of Eve. It is the Nine of Heart's vision that it and the steward can be like higher centers. Pure imagination, and the Nine of Hearts, not the steward, is the first to taste it. Eating the fruit later is simply an outward symbol, a token of an accomplished fact. The Fall is the Nine of Heart's vision of a higher state it can never reach -- eternal presence -- and since it and the steward are one and the same, Eve's taste of pure imagination is the steward's fall also.

East of Eden. Genesis tells us: "3.22 The Lord God said:

'Behold the man has become like one of us, knowing good and evil; and now lest he put forth his hand and take also of the tree of life and eat, and live forever' -- therefore the Lord God sent him forth from the garden of Eden, to till the ground from which he was taken."

What does this passage really mean?

Using the keys "Lord God", "man", "good", "evil" and introducing a new key "life", meaning specifically the steward beginning and completing a sequence, we arrive to an astonishing conclusion: Seeing that the steward and nine of hearts are just like higher centers, knowing as they do the difference between presence and imagination, higher centers let them reach Long BE, but prevent them from experiencing the state of higher emotional presence.

The three divine curses. What happens to the inner state of the steward after falling into imagination to warrant calling it a complete dislocation of its being? First, the King of Clubs and Nine of Hearts begin to work at cross purposes, the "seed of the serpent" (mechanical I's originating in the King of Clubs) and that of Woman (Work I's) become mutually destructive. Secondly, the Nine of Hearts begins to suffer a curious mixture of pain and desire for the steward, this desire leading to misery and pain at giving birth to Work I's. Thirdly, for the first time the steward has to make efforts to be present. The defining property of Eden -- mechanical presence without effort -- ceases to exist.

Passing in and out of imagination, having to make efforts for the first time to remain present, the opposition between the King of Clubs and Nine of Hearts, her insatiable desire, her pain at the birth of Work I's – all these changes signal a profound shift in the psychology of the Nine of Hearts. Even before the burning sword (representing a sequence flaming into Divine Presence) begins to turn, driving them away, the steward and Nine of Hearts are east of Eden.

III. Igniting Higher Emotions

Retrieving the Amduat's third layer. Nearly 30,000 years separate the pre-historic cave paintings inside Chauvet from the hieroglyphic texts with cartoon-like images called *Treatise of the Hidden Chamber* or simply *The Amduat*. Much older than Genesis, these texts and images were painted on the walls of burial chambers of Egyptian pharaohs for nearly 1,500 years.

Another 3,500 years separate those first Amduat paintings from us. And nearly 200 years separate us from the pioneering efforts of Champillion, Young and other Egyptologists to decode the sacred texts. Thanks to their efforts, the second layer of meaning -- metaphor and allegory – has been deciphered. And now thanks to Burton's keys, the third layer is being retrieved.

On a parallel track, the research of Lewis-Williams, Hancock and others is revealing a higher unity: The imagery of pre-historic cave paintings, the imagery of the Amduat (including its hieroglyphics) and, for that matter, Burton's keys may come from the same source: a higher dimension accessed in trance states and populated by the same animals and half-animal/half-humans we see on cave and burial chamber walls.

The allegory: Hour One. The Amduat tells us the Sun God Ra is being greeted on his descent into the Netherworld by a silent Set and a chorus of 84 gods, goddesses and animals. Ra calls to them:

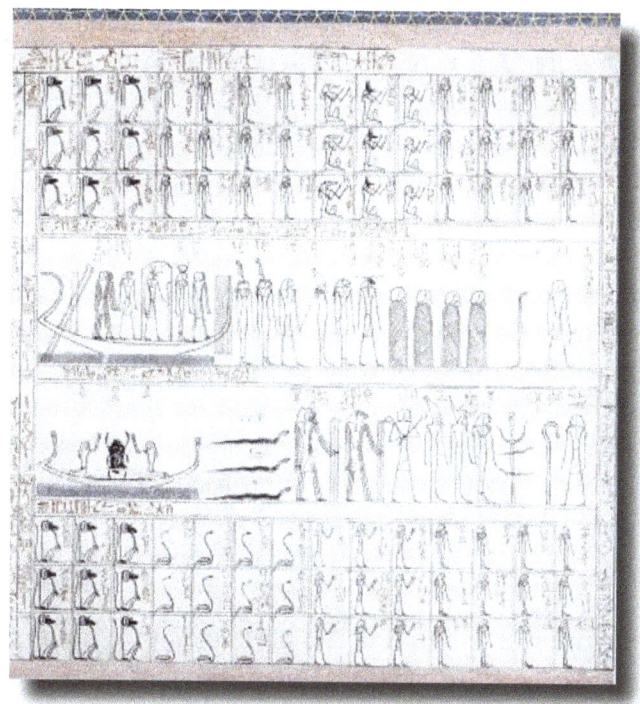

Open your doors for me, open for me your gates. Light up for me, you who were made for me. Guide me, you who came into being out of me. I give you offerings, for you are made out of my body, and I have made you for my soul.

Ra states his purpose in descending:

I come to give [the Breath of Life] to the One Whose Forms Are Hidden, to My Osiris, He at the Head of Those in the West!

Inner meaning of Hour One If the allegory is taken literally, Hour 1 of the Amduat is simply recording a God's movement thru a higher dimension called the Netherworld and his encounter with other Gods there. Complications set in immediately for any reader who is not an Ancient Egyptian and/or does not believe in Sun Gods, the Netherworld and supernatural half-animal/half-humans. The text is still readable, but one becomes estranged from it, it becomes incomprehensible, an anthropological artifact.

Keying the text, one avoids these complications: Whatever the Sun God Ra may or may not have meant to the ancient Egyptian priesthood, we discover in it a hidden meaning for us, it is a key for higher centers, and Ra's descent into the Netherworld a key for higher centers entering the second state. This connects the text immediately to the war going on inside of us. Hour 1 now has psychological immediacy missing before, it is not simply a 4,000 year old artifact.

At this inner level what is the message? Why must higher centers descend into the 2nd state? Why not always remain in a state of presence?.

Hour 1 tells us: Using Work I's and sequences, higher centers (Ra) enter the 2nd state not for themselves, but in order to prolong presence – the four wordless breaths – for the steward (Osiris).

As for the Chorus of 84 Gods, they could represent sequences of Work I's (specifically 14 sequences of 6 Work I's if one does the math).[17] The fact that Ra is greeted by these Gods and these Gods accompany him during his 12-hour journey implies that higher centers are not simply descending into the 2nd state, but entering in some way the

_____

17   The 84 Gods greeting the Sun God could also represent the 72 divisions of the *lower self* plus two sequences of *Work I's* by the steward.

2nd state of Work I's. Are higher centers our outside help whenever our steward invokes Work I's? More on this later.

What about silent Set? Who is he? And why is he of all the Gods greeting Ra? Why not Horus?

Burton has keyed Set as representing the King of Clubs. Seated in the Nine of Clubs, our King of Clubs is controlling the allocation of time and energy to mechanical I's. Located where it is, it is also maintaining the machine's instinctive homeostasis. Could it be this card also regulates the allocation of time and energy for Work I's? Maybe that is why Set, and not Horus (representing the steward) , is at the head of the Chorus of Gods. The King of Clubs cannot invoke Work I's, but it can allocate energy for them once the Work I's have been invoked by the steward.

These considerations regarding Set bring to mind Tarot Card 21, the World Card, showing the Nude Woman (keyed by Burton as representing higher emotional center) being supported by a bull and a lion with a halo. The Bull represents a King of Clubs that accepts the role of supporting higher centers, the Lion With A Halo the steward in a state of presence.

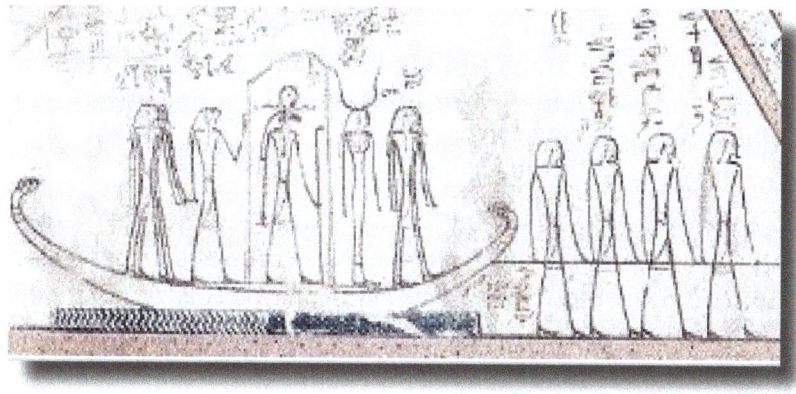

Hour Four: the allegory. The Bark of Ra comes to a standstill inside a cavern called Life of Forms, the Bark's passage is blocked. To travel any farther on the Bark of Ra, Ra must be towed by four gods: He Who Holds the Fore-Rope, He Who Holds the Aft Rope and He Who Stretches the Rope. With an impenetrable darkness everywhere, Ra cannot see nor be seen. He communicates to the gods of the Netherworld with the sound of his voice. He does not see the gods of the Netherworld in their forms nor they him. He calls them, and it is His Word they hear.

Inner meaning of Hour Four. Taken literally, Hour 4 is a beautiful, but unintelligible enigma. Why is the cavern called Life of Forms? And what does Life of Forms mean anyway? Even more strange and distant from us are the names of the four gods towing the Bark of Ra: "Mysterious One, He Who Holds the Fore-Rope, He Who Holds the Aft Rope and He Who Stretches the Rope." What kind of naming is this?

Again, the system of keys proposed here offer readers one possible explanation. The Bark of Ra is a key for the Nine of Hearts. Remember the Nine of Hearts is the site of our emotional intelligence, it is responsible for relativity, scale and emotional discrimination. To say that it has come to a standstill implies that the steward has lost scale and relativity, it has stopped making fine emotional distinctions.

Where this happens is instructive. Burton has not keyed Life of Forms? He has keyed life, however. Life is a metaphor for the movement of the steward completing a sequence and resting at Long BE. And Forms? Work I's seem the most likely candidate. Using Burton's keys and the Table of 72 Functions we discover that the image of the Bark of Ra being stopped in the cavern Life of Forms may be keying the steward and Nine of Hearts stopping in the middle of a sequence. Hour 4 is describing a broken sequence (and its repair).

The allegory tells us that the Bark of Ra has come to a standstill because its passage is being blocked. We are not told what is doing this. Recalling the structure and functioning of sequences, one can hazard a guess: Typically, the steward enters an interval at the 4th step. At this step, the King of Clubs tries to disrupt the sequence. Accordingly, it seems the Nine of Hearts has stopped functioning because of the King of Clubs, represented by Set. However, we discover later (in Hour 7) that the Bark of Ra's path has been blocked by Apopis, and not Set. Apopis keys the Nine of Clubs, the card responsible for maintaining the biological machine's instinctive homeostasis. This is then the denying force to the Nine of Hearts: instinctive homeostasis.

How does the steward bridge this interval?

Using rope imagery, the names of three of the four Gods towing the Bark of Ra quite literally and ingeniously describe the process: "He Who Holds the Fore-Rope, He Who Holds the Aft Rope and He Who Stretches the Rope." The fourth god -- "the Mysterious One" -- seems to be a reminder that the process ultimately transcends description. The names of the god towing Ra's boat are, in fact, keys. He Who Holds the Fore-Rope is a key for Short Be, He Who Holds the Aft Rope a key for Long BE and He Who Stretches the Rope keys the four wordless breaths.

The steward repairs a broken sequence by not getting stuck there, that is, by piercing the veil of imagination closing in on it with another sequence, by renewing its vows a thousand times if necessary Rumi tells us until it reaches Long BE.

Hour Six: the allegory. The 6th hour is the hour of the first rejuvenation called simply the Arrival. In this hour the serpent Many Faces is protecting the body of Ra in His Flesh as He stretches out in the form of Osiris and fuses his head with the feet of Khepri. As Osiris stretches to fuse head-to-feet with Khepri, four groups of four gods stand and witness the rejuvenation – Gods of the Red Crown, Those in Peace, Gods of the White Crown and the Four Breaths.

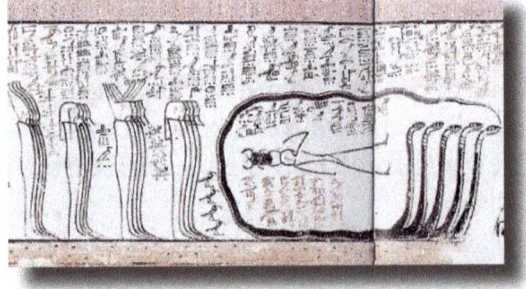

Rejuvenated, Ra speaks through the head of Osiris:

O Radiant One guarding My Image! O Purification of the Gods! May My Image remain hidden! May this darkness become light, and breath enter the members of My Flesh.

The inner meaning. Hour 6 contains perhaps one of the strangest and most striking images in all of sacred literature: a beetle and an outstretched man fusing head-to-head inside a circle formed by a five-headed serpent eating its tail. What does this mean? Another enigma: There are four groups of four gods standing and witnessing this process of fusion -- Gods of the Red Crown, Those in Peace, Gods of the White Crown and the Four Breaths. What is the inner meaning of this imagery?

The beetle representing Khepri keys higher centers, the outstretched man called "Flesh of Ra" and known to the Ancients as Osiris, is a key for the steward. The fusion of these two -- higher centers and the steward -- is a metaphor for the igniting of our higher emotions. Curiously enough, causation is bi-directional: ignition of higher centers resurrects the steward at the same time the steward's resurrection ignites higher centers.

It is no accident that Osiris is stretched out. Osiris stretched out is a key for the steward reaching Long BE, the sixth step in a sequence, and there inhaling and exhaling breaths of wordless presence. The image of a five-headed serpent eating its tail confirms this interpretation: With the five serpent heads representing the first five steps of a sequence, the image of Osiris stretched out and fusing with Khepri is the sixth step.

A second confirmation is found in the text when Ra, speaking thru the head of Osiris, says: "May this darkness become light, and breath enter the members of My Flesh." "May this darkness become light" refers to higher centers igniting and transforming the second state of Work I's into the third state. "[May] breath enter the members of My Flesh" is an explicit, almost literal reference to the steward ("My Flesh") inhaling breaths of presence at Long BE.

As for the four groups of four gods witnessing the fusion and resurrection, the Ancients are reminding us of the supreme importance of presence. Gods of the Red Crown are keys for Short Be, the first Work I of a sequence dispelling imagination. Gods of the White Crown key Long BE while Those in Peace and Four Breaths are keys for the wordless state of presence. But why four groups of four? A pun pointing to a profound mystery: By squaring the four breaths of presence, the Amduat could be suggesting that higher centers reach their own Long BE, analogous to the Long BE reached by the steward, but at the same time light years beyond this state.

IV. Emergence of Higher Intelligence

Hour 7: the allegory continues. Revelations, visionary dreams, prophecy – where do they come from? Perhaps the inner meaning of Hour 7 of the Amduat holds the answer. In the Valley of Kings, on the walls of burial chambers for

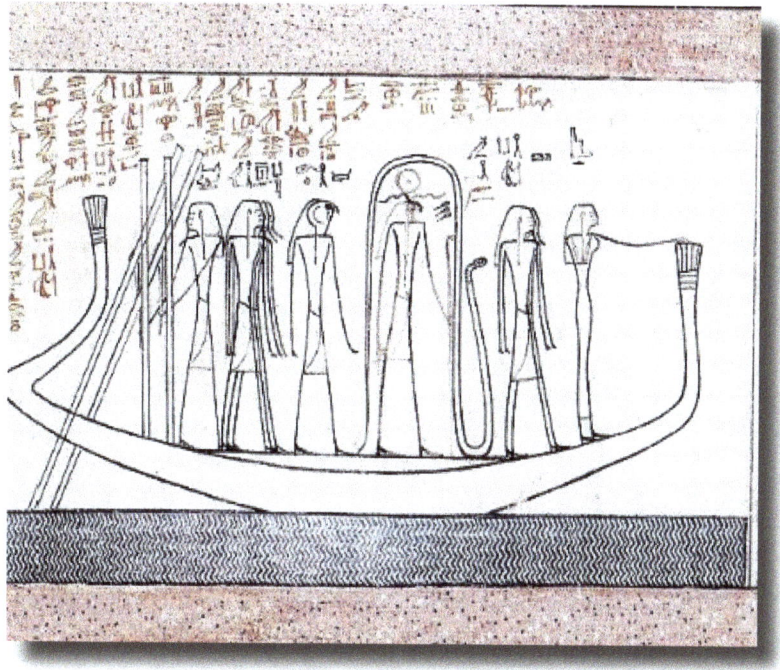

Thutmosis III, Ramses VI and other pharaohs, the events of that crucial hour unfold majestically: The war between Apopis and Ra reaches a crisis point: His solar disk ignited, the Sun God Ra is being powered in a strange new way: the Bark of Ra is moving not by water nor by towing but by

the magic utterances of Isis, Set and the Elder Magician. They are issuing these utterances to repulse Apopis, the One called Evil Face and Loathsome Worm. To do this, Isis, Set and the Elder One ride in the prow of the Bark of Ra uttering magic incantations which deprive Apopis of strength.

Apopis is caught by Selkit, She Who Gives and Cuts off Air In the Wind-pipe. 443 cubits long, Apopis has been transfixed with six knives. At the same time the enemies of Ra are beheaded and the Rebels tied up and chastised. Ra's voice led the gods to Evil Face. Selkit is lassoing him head to tail.

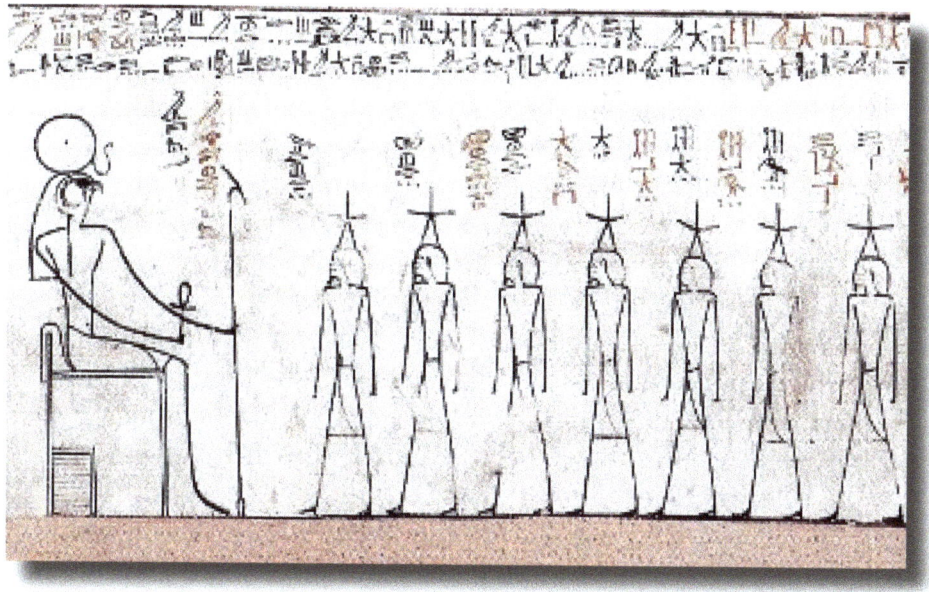

Meanwhile Horus sits on a throne holding a scepter of power in one hand, a life sign in the other. Horus speaks:

O gods of the starry hours,
May your flesh be right...
May your forms come into being...
You are content indeed with your stars!

Stand up before Ra, He of
the Horizon. You are in
his following while your stars are before him
to let him pass to
the beautiful West in peace.
Your stars belong to me, and I who am
in Heaven am content.

The inner meaning. In this context, "ignited" means the higher emotional center is starting to function, it is combusting. The "magic utterances of Isis, etc." are not sequences of the steward, they are sequences of Work I's coming directly from the Nine of Hearts, and "magic" is a key for higher emotions transforming the shock of each effort of a Work I directly into presence. This continual transformation of shocks into presence by the higher emotional center deprives the King of Clubs of the energy and will to resist and sabotage the steward. The King of Clubs is "caught" and "lassoed head to tail", meaning the King of Clubs is finally being mastered by the higher emotional center -- not by the steward. The King of Clubs has become the Bull without a Halo supporting the Dancing Woman on Tarot Card 21. "Transfixed with 6 knives" is a key for the paralyzing effect on the King of Clubs of a sequence of 6 Work I's coming directly from the higher emotional center.

Do revelations and visionary dreams originate here: In a combusting higher emotional center with a paralyzed transfixed King of Clubs completely immobilized by Work I's – six knives from the Nine of Hearts?

"Horus on a throne" is a key for the steward celebrating the ascension of higher emotional center. His song is a song of thanksgiving: "O gods of the starry hours", Horus sings: "May your
flesh be right...May your forms come into being..."

Is this the true role of the steward: To not be an active force itself, to step aside and sing praises to the ascending higher emotions?

"Gods of the starry hours" are Work I's passing through our 2nd state, sometimes in the form of sequences, more often singly. And then there are those exceptional occasions when Work I's can "stand up before Ra". Then higher emotional center is functioning. Horus the steward sings: "You are in his following while your stars are before him to let him pass to the beautiful West in peace."

"Let him pass to the beautiful West in peace" is a key for Long BE and the 4 wordless breaths. But note: this is the Long BE of higher emotional center, and not the Long BE of the steward. Higher emotional center is on the threshold of giving birth to its Wordless Companion, higher intellectual center.

Hour Ten – the allegory. The Amduat tells us: The Eye of Ra is coming out of the two heads of the Double-Entwined One as the goddesses of the Red and White Crown look on and channel the Eye of Ra with their index fingers into their Third

Eyes. The Eye of Horus is emerging from a god hieroglyph called He Who Does The Fastening, and two goddesses -- The One Who Lifts Up and The One Who Calls God – are channeling the Eye of Horus through their hands. The Double-Entwined One and He Who Does The Fastening call to "souls over the face of the earth" to join them, and these souls come, "fastening themselves to this mysterious image of the Eyes of Ra and Horus, inhaling the image and purifying their radiant breaths in the Netherworld."

Inner meanings. Hour 10 is the hour of rebirth of higher centers, the hour of revelation: The Eye of Ra coming out

of the two-headed serpent Double-Entwined One is a metaphor for higher intelligence of World 6 emerging from a pair of sequences, one from the steward, the other from higher emotional center. The fact that the goddesses of the Red and White Crown are looking on and channeling the Eye of Ra with their index fingers into their Third Eyes simply highlights being in its two forms (Short and Long BE) in the emergence of higher intelligence. As for higher emotional center, its image is an enigma: higher emotions are somehow resting on the hieroglyph for God. What could this mean? At the same time, the emotions are being attended by two strange goddesses -- the One Who Calls God and the One
Who Lifts Up. Could this represent higher emotions at the end of a sequence?

The imagery of the text in this strange hour shows the two entwined serpents and the God hieroglyph attracting all souls from the face of the earth. As they arrive, the souls become "fastened" to images of the Third Eye, inhaling and purifying their breaths. What are the ancient Egyptians trying to communicate?

The revelation itself.

We know already "soul" keys the steward. Like the Red and White crowns, could the Double-Entwined serpents also represent the two forms of being? And like the word "God", could the God hieroglyph key higher centers also? The meaning of this final image hinges on the meaning of "fastening".

Yes, on at least two levels of meaning comprehensible to us: "Fastening" means the soul's higher emotions connecting momentarily or permanently with its higher intelligence to receive higher knowledge. The mystical marriage and sexual union of higher centers. And "fastening" also means higher centers connecting with Influence C to receive this knowledge. A divine orgasm. There are higher levels of meaning we cannot comprehend, such as we are.

Hour Twelve: the allegory. The Bark of Ra is towed into the tail of a serpent 1300 cubits long called Life of the Gods. The Sun God on board and his crew travel along the backbone of the serpent and come out of its mouth as Khepri rejuvenated. Those who are aged and honored by Ra enter the serpent's backbone also and come out of its mouth the Youth of Ra.

Twelve turquoise blue gods celebrate Khepri's ascent into the dawn sky. They sing: "Born is he who is born, came into being, he who has come into being. Your sky is for your Soul to rest in, the Earth for Your Body, O Lord of Glory! mount the horizon!"As the Bark comes out of the serpent's mouth, thirteen goddesses take hold of the Nefert-rope and tow the Bark into the sky.

Osiris, the Body of Ra, remains behind residing in darkness. "Live! Live!" gods of the procession tell Osiris, "The breath of Ra is for your nostrils. The breathing of Khepri is before you. You live the life of the living. Hail, Osiris, lord of life!"

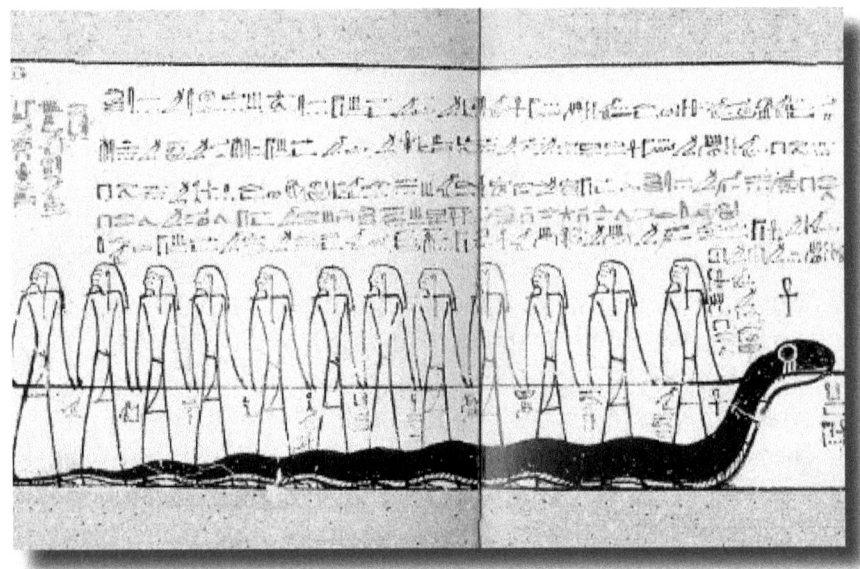

The inner meaning. Keying the Bark of Ra discloses the Nine of Hearts. The fact that it is being towed into the tail of a serpent 1300 cubits long called Life of the Gods alerts us to the fact that the Nine of Hearts is at the end of its role, and not the beginning. The Sun God keys higher centers, the crew on board Work I's issuing directly from higher centers.

Higher emotions are combusting already, but a payment must be made even here. The Nine of Hearts must die. Its death signals the regeneration and rebirth of higher centers. There is no other way.

To repeat, what comes at the end of a sequence now comes at its beginning. The Nine of Hearts is dead, long live the Nine of Hearts. Higher emotions have been ignited, higher intelligence has emerged, both are functioning intertwined and fastened together in two states of Presence, but the Nine of Hearts has become Osiris, remaining behind entombed in the darkness of the 2nd state -- literally a Recurring Life-in-Death.

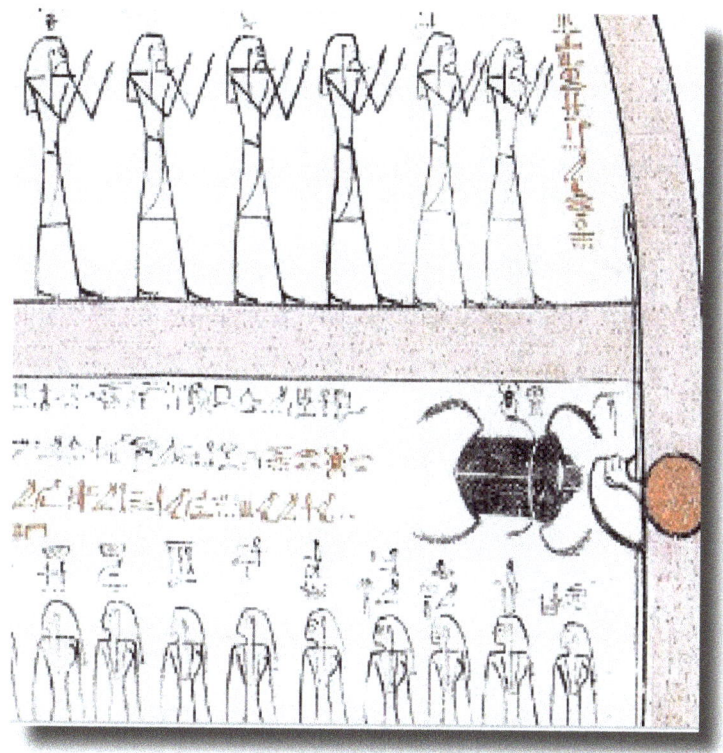

The hymn of the turquoise blue gods is then a Hymn to Presence. They sing: "Born is he who is born" meaning higher emotions have ignited, "Came into being, he who has come into being", meaning this time higher intelligence has emerged and is functioning. "Your sky is for your Soul to rest in". "Rest" and 'sky' are both keys for presence, and "soul" a key for higher centers. "The Earth [is] for Your Body", the turquoise blue gods sing. Earth keys the 2nd state, and Body is a key for the Nine of Hearts at the end of its role.

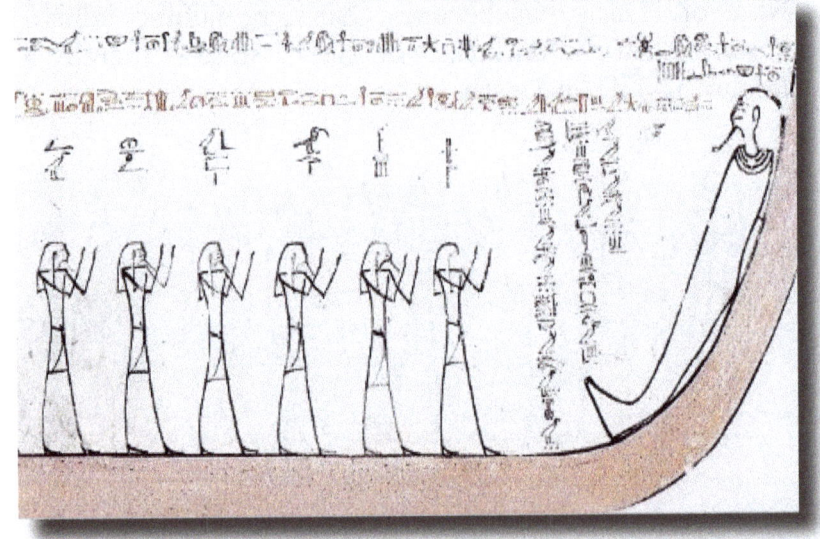

V. Losing One's Wings

Plato's winged chariot driver. In Hour 4 of the Amduat we encounter perhaps the earliest recorded imagery for a broken sequence: In a cavern called Life of Forms Apopis dries up the Waters of Osiris, forcing four lesser Gods to tow the Bark of Ra by hand across hot desert sand.

In the Phaedrus some 1200 years later we encounter another allegory dealing with broken sequences. Here Plato likens it to a winged charioteer who is driving winged horses to keep up with the Gods, but in the effort damages, breaks off and loses both his wings and those of his horses, plummeting to Earth.

How is this possible?

"The natural property of a wing," Plato tells us, "is to raise that which is heavy and carry it aloft to the region where the Gods dwell. More than any other bodily part it shares in the divine nature, it is beautiful, wise, good and possessed of all other such excellences." How then does it become broken off?

To begin with, "soul" is a key for steward, and in relation to the steward, Plato is describing the properties of a sequence of Work I's reaching completion. Compared to the 10,000 mechanical I's, each sequence brings the steward as close as it will ever get to higher centers without becoming higher centers.

But then there are times when "close" is not close enough. The sequence can be broken, even at the 6th step. The steward can lose his wings and fall.

How does this happen?

Plato explains: "By ugliness and evil, [the wing] is wasted and destroyed." (Plato, 246e) "Ugliness" is a key for the expression of negative emotion and "evil" for imagination. Imagination and the expression of negative emotions waste away and destroy the effectiveness of sequences, eventually these "break" and "fall off".

The Greek Gods: Higher centers, stewards, or lower centers? And what about the Gods? Greek Gods are an enigma. In Genesis we found that "God" is a key for higher centers, Presence, and in the Amduat and other sacred Egyptian

texts we discover the Ancients careful to distinguish between the "Supreme God" Ra (a.k.a. the Divine Beetle Khepri), and the lesser ruling Gods: Osiris, Isis, Nepthys, Horus, Set, Thoth, Anubis, Apopis. Like the God of the Old and New Testaments the Sun God is a key for presence and higher centers. Its synonyms are Third Eye, Eye of Ra, Eye of Horus. The lesser gods, on the other hand, are metaphors for the steward if male divinities (Osiris, Horus, Anubis), and the Nine of Hearts if female. The two exceptions: Set, He Who Tears Everything to Pieces, and Apopis, the Loathsome Worm, are keys for the King of Clubs and lower self. A neat and logically tidy universe.

Turn to the Greek Gods: that neat and tidy universe of the Ancient Egyptians collapses into a world of gods that are still immortal, but all too human: bloodthirsty combative Ares, for example, inspires men to settle accounts with the fist or the sword, a sexually promiscuous Aphrodite fills men, women and animals with an insatiable erotic desire, a wine and hallucinogenic-drinking Dionysus inspires men and women to enter ecstatic, sometimes orgiastic trance states, and Zeus the Supreme God himself, becoming sexually aroused, loses all self-control, and seduces his own wife in a luminous cloud.[2]

Depicted as they are by Homer, Hesiod and Pindar, can the Gods of the Ancient Greeks still be considered keys for higher centers and the steward?. Not as they are: raw, unpurified forms of essence. Not so much higher centers or stewards, the Ancient Greek Gods seem more like metaphors for the ruling parts of our biological machines: Zeus, Aphrodite and Eros, for example, representing different aspects of the sex center, Dionysus and Ares being keys for the King of Clubs, Apollo the King of Diamonds, and Athena and Diana the Nine of Hearts.

Heracleitus speaks out. In the 6th century BC, expressing his chagrin over the rituals of the followers of Dionysus, Heraclitus of Ephesus had this to say:

> *Dionysus is their name for death.*
> *And if they did not claim*
> *the statute of the drunk*
> *they worshipped was a god,*
> *or call their incoherent song*
> *about his cock their hymn,*
> *everyone would know*
> *what filth their shamelessness*
> *has made of them*
> *and of the name of God.*[3]

Plato's radical surgery purifying the imagery of Gods. Less caustic, Plato is no less severe in his criticism of Homer and Hesiod. "To represent the wisest man [Odysseus] as saying that this seems to him the fairest thing in the world, 'When bounteous tables are standing laden with bread and with meat, etc' do you think the hearing of that sort of thing will conduce to temperance or self control? ... Or to hear how Zeus lightly forgot all his designs...because of the excitement of his sexual desire, and was so overcome by the sight of Hera that he is not even willing to go to their chamber, but wants to lie with her there and then on the ground..."[4] Plato's solution: Purify the imagery of Gods by excising morally offensive passages from the works of Homer, Hesiod and other poets.

In the Phaedrus Plato presents the results of his radical surgery: "Behold, there in heaven, Zeus, mighty leader, drives his winged team. First of the host of gods and daemons he proceeds, ordering and caring therefore..., and the host follows after him marshaled in eleven companies." These are the Gods of Homer and Hesiod in name only as we soon discover. Plato writes: "Now within the heavens are many spectacles of bliss upon the highways whereon the blessed gods pass to and fro, each doing his work, and with them all such as will and can follow them, for jealousy has no place in the choir divine."

The surgeon's knife has cut away the offending tissue: "Each doing his work" means the competitiveness and intrigue in Homer's depiction has been removed. Even more drastically, jealousy no longer has a place. This is Plato's vision of the Gods, not the Gods of the Theogony or Illiad.

What has Plato done?

Reviving the ancient teaching. Plato, a student of the Egyptian Mysteries, is reviving an ancient hermetic teaching with roots in Egypt, predating the conventional Greek view of his times by thousands of years: Higher centers in their purity do not under any circumstances have or ever express negative emotions, greed or lust, there is no competitiveness, no jealousy, only arête, only pure virtue, continuous, uninterrupted sequences of Work I's.[5]

Plato continues: "But at such times as they go to their feasting and banquet, behold they climb the steep ascent even unto the summit of the arch that supports the heavens, and easy is that ascent for the chariot of the gods, for they are well balanced and readily guided.

But for the others it is hard, by reason of the heaviness of the steed of wickedness, which pulls down his driver with his weight...". Plato the visionary is reminding us that he is also Plato the teacher, guiding us to a new revelation: The Gods are winged charioteers also, but immortal. Such as they are in their original goodness, purified of human brutality, the Gods are keys for higher centers prolonging presence continuously.

"The summit of the arch that supports the heavens" is a key for prolonging presence with four wordless breaths. By not being pulled down by the "heaviness" of imagination, higher centers continually reach Long BE and higher states without difficulty.

Plato's imagery of these higher states is no less extraordinary than his vision of what higher centers completing sequences "see" there. "For the souls that are called immortal [i.e., higher centers], so soon as they are at the summit, come forth and stand upon the back of the world, and straightway the revolving heaven carries them round, and they look upon the regions without." What a strange image: higher centers coming to a standstill and revolving with the heavens to view a region beyond heaven itself. What do they "see" there?

"Of that place beyond heaven none of our earthly poets have yet sung...But this is the manner of it: It is there that true being dwells, without color or shape, it cannot be touched; reason alone, the soul's pilot, can behold it, and all true knowledge is knowledge thereof.... wherefore when at last [higher centers] has beheld being, well content, and contemplating truth she is nourished and prospers, until the heavens revolution brings her back full circle. And while she is carried around she discerns justice and likewise temperance, and knowledge"

"Reason, the soul's pilot" is a key for higher intellectual center, "true being" a key for presence., and "seeing" a key for remembering and being present .

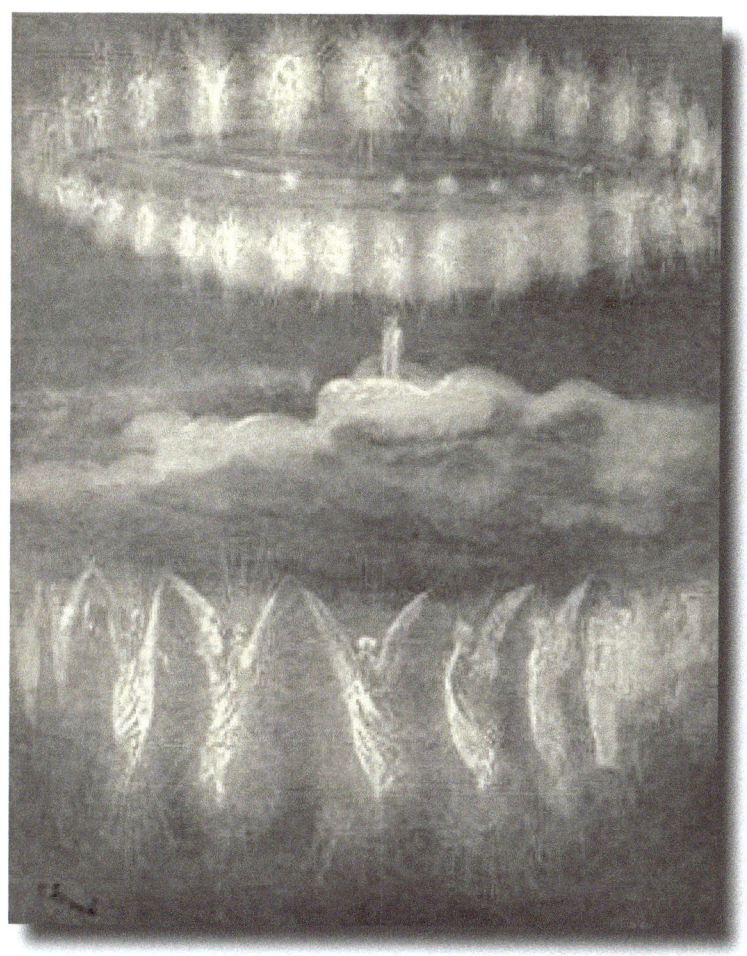

Plato is telling us that higher centers are using their higher
intelligence, 'the soul's pilot", to see what they, in fact, are:
their own presence -- they are remembering and being
present to it. Plato has many names for presence: "virtues"
(justice, temperance, knowledge, etc). We call them
"Work I's". At this highest level of being, higher centers
see themselves as they are thru and thru: the presence of
uncontaminated, uncreated absolute goodness.[6]

Illusions of presence. Plato's vision of higher centers is quite different from his vision of the fate awaiting mortal souls, i.e., stewards of Men No. 4 and 5. In the Phaedrus, even the most conscientious mortal soul following closely behind a God reaches the summit (the 4th state) only to be pulled down again and as a result receives only a partial glimpse of "true being".

"By reason of her unruly steeds [kings of lower centers resisting or interrupting sequences], [the steward who makes efforts consistently] sees in part, but in part sees not."

As for the rest," Plato observes, "though all are eager to reach the heights and seek to follow [a God], they cannot. Sucked down as they travel, [kings of lower centers] trample and tread upon one another, this one striving to outstrip that. Thus confusion ensues, and conflict and grievous sweat. Whereupon, with their charioteers [stewards] powerless, many are lamed, and many have their wings all broken, and for their toiling they are balked, every one, of the full vision of being, and departing therefrom, they feed upon the food of semblance." Plato is recounting the inner state of the ruling parts of biological machines – the kings and queens of lower centers -- in varying degrees of sleep, sometimes waking momentarily, but even then being too weak and unreliable to ascend. So pathetic, it may even be going too far to call them "stewards". Like powerless charioteers, they look on helplessly as a succession of mechanical I's, passing thru the kings and queens of centers, "trample and tread upon one another." Denied even a partial momentary glimpse of presence, these kings ofcenters must feed on the "food of semblance", meaning the illusion of presence, imagination

Plato's cave: a metaphor for imagination. In Book VII of *The Republic* Plato gives a detailed description of this illusion. "Picture men dwelling in a sort of underground cave", he writes, "With a long entrance open to the light on its entire length. Conceive them as having their legs and necks chained from childhood, so that they remain in the same spot, able to look forward only, and prevented by the chains from turning their heads."

Plato's "underground cave" is a key for imagination, "legs and necks" represent the intellectual parts of centers, "chains" our "A-Influence programming, and "turning their heads" a key for completing a sequence and remembering oneself. Plato is inviting us to consider the inner state and psychology of stewards blocked from birth by their programming from completing sequences and remembering themselves.

"Picture the light from a fire burning higher up and at a distance behind [the prisoners]", Plato writes. "[Picture] Between the fire and the prisoners and above them a road along which a low wall has been built...and see men carrying past the wall implements of all kinds that rise above the wall, and human images and shapes of animals, wrought in stone and wood and every material, some presumably speaking and others silent [casting shadows on the wall in front of them]." The "fire burning higher up" is another key for imagination. Plato is describing a virtual reality being generated by mechanical I's in imagination ("the men carrying" images) all the time. Plato asks rhetorically: "Do you think these men ould have seen anything of themselves or one another except the shadows cast from the fire onto the wall of the cave in front of them?" Answering his own question, Plato observes: "In every way such prisoners would deem reality to be nothing else than shadows of artificial objects". Programmed from birth to view the virtual reality generated by their own mechanical I's as reality, unable to remember themselves even momentarily and so unable to catch a glimpse of divine presence as it really is, most stewards come to view imagination -- the illusion of presence -- as presence itself.

The steward re-growing its wings. "What would be the manner of the release and healing from these chains?" Plato is asking about the four wordless breaths, and he answers: "When one is freed from his chains and compelled to stand up suddenly and turn his head around and walk and lift his eyes to the light, [the steward feels] pain" and is unable "to discern the objects whose shadows he formerly saw" because of "the dazzle and glitter of the light." Disorienting, even to the point

of pain, but nonetheless promoting the healing of one's "wings", the steward slowly accustoms itself to making efforts to be present. Here "eyes" are a key for intellectual parts of centers and "light" a key for presence.

And "the sun"? This is no image of Apollo, no metaphor for the ruling part of the intellectual center. No, in The Phaedrus and The Republic "the sun" is Ra, unnamed by Plato, but functioning in the same way as the ancient Egyptian key for higher centers, and "its true nature" a key for presence.

VI. Noisy gong or clanging cymbal...

A quantum leap for hermetic teachings. A third of the way through the first century AD an itinerant Jewish carpenter named Jesus of Nazareth began gathering a small band of followers and practicing a teaching that soon became the basis for a strange new religion called Christianity. Roman authorities tried as best they could to buffer and avoid contact with these early Christians, but to no avail. Practicing a doctrine called "seeking after death", for example, a few extremists in the group (a minority it seems) "goaded, chided, belittled and insulted [Roman] crowds until [the latter] demanded their death." In one instance, a group "presented themselves to the Roman governor of Asia, C. Arrius Antoninus, declared themselves to be Christians, and encouraged the governor to do his duty and put them to death. He executed a few, but as the rest demanded it as well, he responded, exasperated, "You wretches, if you want to die,
you have cliffs to leap from and ropes to hang by."

What was happening?

Antoninus and other Roman authorities did not know -- and perhaps could not know -- that these and thousands of other early Christians were practicing at the literal level a new and profoundly different paradigm of religion: passive nonviolent resistance to repression as an act of higher emotional love. So powerful was this form of civil disobedience that nearly 300 years later and after the torture and executions of tens of thousands Roman citizens, the Roman empire's wheels of repression simply stopped turning, falling to pieces nonviolently, and an empire of millions was converted en masse and without bloodshed to Christianity.

Two thousand years later under vastly different circumstances on opposite sides of the planet the same effect was produced from the same cause, first in India in the nonviolent resistance movement of Mahatma Gandhi called satyagraha and then in civil rights movement led by Martin Luther King in the U.S.

What kind of religious teaching could produce so profound an effect on humanity? One possible answer: 1) a teaching whose literal meaning eats away false personality and in so doing undermines the prevailing rituals of society, and 2) a teaching whose inner meaning appeals directly to the deeply buried moral conscience of humanity and in so doing ignites the higher emotion of love.

Leaving aside a discussion of satyagraha for now and focusing on the teachings implicit in the nonviolent resistance movements of early Christians and their modern civil rights descendents, let's go directly to the crux of the matter: the Gospels of the New Testament (including the gnostic Gospels of Thomas and Judas).[7] There we find at the literal level a profoundly unsettling vision of love and betrayal, a vision running contrary it seems to common sense, a vision unparalleled in the history of humanity, and at the inner level a small quantum leap in our understanding of higher centers and
their origin that relocates hermetic teachings to another plane. On both levels, the Gospels (orthodox and gnostic) represent the hinge of history, the narrow door to presence swinging back and forth on the pegs of time.

The orthodox teaching. The Gospels are an unusual set of sacred documents: Tucked inside its outer orthodox teaching on higher emotional love, there is an inner Gnostic teaching recounting the origin of Influence C and higher centers. The outer teaching is for humanity generally, it is designed for agnostics, magnetic centers unsure of themselves, uncertain which path to follow, sincerely religious and pious men and women of all faiths with a desire, however faint and intermittent, to become one with the Divine Presence. This outer teaching involves training the steward, teaching it to simply be. Even though its prescriptions have a profound inner meaning, the outer circle of humanity often understands the teaching literally -- with explosive, and sometimes revolutionary, social consequences. It is designed to destroy literal, formatory ways of thinking.

Matthew 5:38: "You have heard that it was said: 'An eye for an eye and a tooth for a tooth. But I say to you, Do not resist one who is evil. But if any one strikes you on the right cheek, turn to him the other also." A first time reader of this passage is stunned: Is there some mistake? What could the author possibly mean? At the literal level, does it mean I let robbers break in at night, plunder my house, abuse and molest my wife and children, and offer no resistance if I am able to? Nonsense. Even at the inner level something is missing. "Evil" we have learned is a key for imagination, and "you" keys the steward. Is the inner meaning of this passage suggesting that the steward should not resist imagination, not stop a mechanical I based entirely on imagination? More nonsense?

Luke 6:27: "But I say to you that hear, Love your enemies, do good to those who hate you, bless those who curse you, pray for those who abuse you. To him who strikes you on the cheek, offer the other also." Another enigma for the shocked first time reader: Literally, is one being asked to love the men who are abusing and molesting one's wife and children? Unthinkable.

What about the inner meaning of this passage? Does that make any more sense?

"Love" has been keyed in its verb form to mean "be present" and in its noun form to mean simply "presence". "Enemies" keys mechanical I's opposing presence. "Hate", the opposite of love, is another key for imagination, but also for negative emotions, which are driven more often than not by negative imagination, by insane mechanical I's making blind semi-psychotic connections.

At the inner level then, Luke's instructions are telling the steward within to be present to mechanical I's in imagination and opposing presence, to be passive to these I's and simply continue to be present (the inner meaning of "do good"). At this level, the passage begins to make a little sense, not much, since instructing the steward to be present to mechanical I's in imagination without itself falling into imagination seems infinitely easier to say than do.

Luke 6:35: At last we find the loose end of a thread for unraveling these enigmas: "Love your enemies and do good," Luke tells us, ".... and you will be sons of the Most High; for he is kind to the ungrateful and the selfish. Be merciful even as your Father is merciful." The reason for the steward loving its enemy (the lower self and King of Clubs) is simple: In this way it can become a mirror-image of higher centers. No longer the God of justice, of an eye for an eye, of Karmic balance, higher centers are a loving pair, merciful, kind, generous, being present to good and evil indifferently even as the sun shines on the criminal and his victim indifferently.

The implications are revolutionary. For the first time in the history of hermetic teachings the unconditional loving nature of higher centers becomes the basis for the steward's inner psychological work. Higher centers were always this way -- merciful, kind, generous unconditionally --, Plato was beginning to see this, but to base the psychology of the steward squarely on this fact requires a radical shift in one's attitude and thinking about good (presence) and evil (imagination), some might say, a rupture and break.

Unraveling the enigmas. Returning to the Gospel of Matthew, we can attempt to unravel one of the enigmas: "You have heard that it was said: 'An eye for an eye and a tooth for a tooth . But I say to you, Do not resist one who is evil, etc." From the mountain top of nonviolent movements scaled by early Christian martyrs and two thousand years later by MK Gandhi, ML King and their followers, humanity now understands Jesus' injunction to not resist one who is evil. Jesus is enjoining us to not resist evil with evil, hatred with hatred, violence with violence, but to resist violence (mechanical I's culminating sooner or later in the expression of negative emotion) with non-violence (sequences of work I's culminating in presence), evil (imagination) with good (four wordless breaths of presence), hatred (negative emotions) with love (the higher emotion of presence). Resist by manifesting the God Within.

Based on this relocation of the steward's inner work, the outer teaching in the Gospels reduces the ten commandments to two: 'You (the steward) shall love (be present to) the Lord your God (higher centers) with all your heart (the nine of hearts), and with all your soul (all yourself -- the steward), and with all your mind (the Nine of Hearts). This is the great and first commandment. And a second is like it. You (the steward) shall love [be present to] your neighbor (another steward) as yourself [steward]. On these two commandments depend all the law (work Is) and the prophets (stewards)."

Corinthians 13:1. In his letter to the Corinthians Paul summarizes the outer teaching in one of the most profoundly moving visions of higher emotional love ever written. He writes: "If I speak in the tongues of men and angels, but have not love, I am a noisy gong or a clanging cymbal. And if I have prophetic powers, and understand all mysteries and all knowledge, and if I have all faith, so as to remove mountains, but have not love, I am nothing..." 13:4. "Love is patient and kind; love is not jealous or boastful; it is not arrogant or rude. Love does not insist on its own way; it is not irritable or resentful; it does not rejoice at wrong, but rejoices in the right. Love bears all things, believes all things, hopes all things, endures all things..." 13:11. "When I was a child, I spoke like a child, I thought like a child, I reasoned like a child; when I became a man, I gave up childish ways. For now we see in a mirror dimly, but then face to face. Now I know in part; then I shall understand fully even as I have been fully understood. So faith, hope, love abide, these three; but the greatest of these is love."

Keying the above passage reveals a vision of the steward's efforts profoundly different on the surface, but nevertheless rooted in the ancient teaching. According to Burton, "If I speak in the tongues of men and angels" refers to the steward making efforts to complete a sequence. "But have not love" is a key for the steward doing this in imagination and without presence. Paul writes further: "And if I have prophetic powers, and understand all mysteries and all knowledge, and if I have all faith, so as to remove mountains, but have not love, I am nothing..." According to Burton, "prophetic powers" are keying the steward's capacity to set the aim of completing a sequence and then completing it. But this ability to complete a sequence is meaningless, Paul tells us, if I "have not love", that is, if the steward completes the sequence in imagination and without presence.

In 13.4 Paul describes the nature of higher emotional love, true on many levels: "Love is patient and kind; love is not jealous or boastful; it is not arrogant or rude. Love does not insist on its own way; it is not irritable or resentful; it does not rejoice at wrong, but rejoices in the right. Love bears all things, believes all things, hopes all things, endures all things..." According to Burton, higher emotional love keys the presence of higher centers, but since this is one of those rare instances in sacred literature when what is true at the inner level, is also true at other levels, including the literal, presence keys higher emotional love: Higher centers for sure, but even the steward in a state of presence, is "patient and kind", "not arrogant or rude", "not irritable or resentful" etc.

In 13.11 Paul describes the maturation of the steward from its infancy as an Observing I in essence to a mature steward completing sequences. "When I was a child, I spoke like a child, etc." refers to the steward seeing and knowing in state of essence without presence.

"When I became a man, I gave up childish ways" keys the mature steward. "For now we see in a mirror dimly" describes the steward in imagination. "But then face to face" keys the steward in a state of presence.

The Gnostic inner teaching. The orthodox teaching is a training ground for humanity generally, it focuses on the primacy of higher emotional love. The gnostic teaching, on the other hand, presupposes this training. Intended for the inner circle of humanity – for its prophets, spiritual teachers and advanced souls generally, it focuses on the origin and nature of higher centers. Incomprehensible to the average steward, hidden from the outer circle of humanity by layers of metaphor and allegory, misunderstood even when it is revealed, this teaching is from higher centers, and for higher centers.

John 1:1-4. Appearing in the orthodox canon of Gospels, John 1:1-4 is nevertheless a fragment from this Gnostic teaching: "In the beginning was the Word, and the Word was with God, and the Word was God...In Him was life, and the life was the light of men. The light shines in the darkness, and the darkness has not understood it."

Keying the above passage, we see for the first time a reference to higher centers and their origin in the Absolute: "In the beginning [At the start of a sequence] was the Word [Be], and the Word was with God [the Absolute], and the Word was God...In Him was life [higher centers], and the life was the light of men [eternal presence]. The light [presence] shines in the darkness [2nd state of the steward], and the darkness has not understood it."

John 15:4 Jesus (speaking to his disciples): "Abide in me, and I in you. As the branch cannot bear fruit by itself, unless it abides in the vine, neither can you, unless you abide in me 15:9-10. As the Father has loved me, so have I loved you, abide in my love. If you keep my commandments, you will abide in my love, just as I have kept my Father's commandments and abide in his love." 15:12. "This is my commandment: that you love one another as I have loved you.

In 15.4 we get another glimpse into the inner teaching of the Gnostics, this time expressed in terms of a teacher instructing members of his inner circle. The tone is personal, even intimate. This is no Sermon on the Mount, no breaking of bread for thousands, but Jesus instructing his inner circle literally to be present to him. "Abide in me, and I in you", he tells them. If one interprets this passage using the keys for the outer teaching, this is simply one steward speaking to others. Be present to me a steward as I am to you other stewards. But the passage goes to a much deeper level. As part of the inner teaching of the Gnostics, John 15:4 is exploring the relationship of the steward to higher centers and higher centers to the Absolute.

"Abide in me and I in you". Keying this passage in terms of the inner teaching, one arrives at a profoundly different understanding: steward, be present to higher centers and let higher centers be present to you. Similarly, the passage "As the Father has loved me , so have I loved you, abide in my love. If you keep my commandments, you will abide in my love, just as I have kept my Father's commandments and abide in his love" takes on a fundamentally different meaning. Here "Father" keys the Absolute, "I" is a key for higher centers, and "you" keys the steward. With these keys, another level of meaning is exposed: As the Absolute is present to higher centers, in the same way higher centers are present to the steward. For this reason, the steward must remain present to higher centers.

Thomas 94:23. The Gospel of Thomas touches briefly on the cosmology of higher centers and their origin: "Jesus said: I am the Light that is above them all, I am the All, the All came from Me, and the All stretches as far as Me, and no farther. Split a piece of wood, I am there; lift up a stone and you will find Me there."

Keying this passage, we witness higher emotions transmitting hydrogen 12 from Influence C (the Light), i.e., that state of higher centers nearest to stewards (World 12), and combusting into the lower world of biological functions while higher intelligence transmits Influence C with an even finer hydrogen (World 6): "Jesus said: I [higher centers] am the Light [eternal presence] that is above them all, I am the All [Worlds 6, 12, 24 and the five lower centers], the All came from Me, and the All stretches as far as Me, and no farther. Split a piece of wood [Start a sequence with Short Be], I am there; lift up a stone [complete a sequence and reach Long BE]and you will find Me there."[8]

Other passages from the Gospel of Thomas confirm the transcendent nature of higher centers:

Thomas 95:17. Jesus said: Whoever is near to me [higher centers] is near to the fire [eternal presence], and whoever is far from me is far from the Kingdom [eternal presence]

Thomas 95:20. "Images [Work I's] are revealed to man [the steward] and the light within them [presence] is hidden in the Image of the Light [eternal presence] of the Father[the Absolute]."

Thomas 89:31. "Jesus said: If they say to you: 'From where have you [higher centers] originated?', say to them: We have come from the Light [eternal presence], where the Light originates from itself [higher centers]."

Thomas 90:2. "If they say to you: 'Who are you?', say: 'We [higher centers] are the elect of the Living Father [the Absolute]'. If they ask you: 'What is the sign of your Father in you?', say to them: 'It is a movement [a sequence using the steward from Short Be thru Middle Be to Long BE]] and a rest [four wordless breaths] .'"

The Gnostic inner teaching finally re-connects with the orthodox outer teaching: Higher centers are presence, and presence is higher emotional love: Thomas 86:26. "Jesus said: Love thy brother (higher centers, be present

to each other) as thy soul (your own steward), guard him as the apple of thine eye."

John 16:27. "For the Father himself (the Absolute) loves you (is present to your higher centers) because you (stewards) have loved me (been present to my higher centers) and have believed (accepted as true without verification) that I came from the Father (that higher centers came from the Absolute).."

VII. Gospel of the thirteenth disciple

"Jesus said: The Pharisees and the Scribes have received the keys of Knowledge, but they have hidden them. They did not enter, and they did not let those enter who wished to enter."

Gospel of Thomas 88:39

A luminous cloud. Near the conclusion of The Gospel of Judas we are presented a strange and arresting image. Jesus is instructing Judas: "Lift up your eyes and look at the cloud and the light within it and the stars surrounding it. The star that leads the way is your star."⁹ The narrator tells us that Judas obeyed Jesus, he "lifted up his eyes and saw the luminous cloud, and he entered it." What is the meaning of this passage?

Earlier Jesus had prophesized Judas' fate, "You will become the thirteenth, and you will be cursed by the other generations -- and you will come to rule over them. In the last days they will curse your ascent to the holy." What does this prophesy mean?

Judas is in grief, not wanting to be despised and cast out by the other disciples. Knowing this, Jesus tries to console him, explaining what it means to be the thirteenth disciple and revealing a cosmology tracing the divinity of Jesus and Judas back to the Absolute before the Creation described in Genesis. Step away from the others," Jesus tells Judas, "And I shall tell you the mysteries of the kingdom."

Judas 87. There exists a great and boundless realm whose

extent no generation of angels has seen, [in which] there is [a] great invisible [Spirit] which no eye of an angel has ever seen, no thought of the heart has ever comprehended, and it was never called by any name. There a luminous cloud appeared. [The Invisible Spirit] said: 'Let an angel come into being as my attendant.

Judas 93. A great angel, the enlightened divine Self-Generated, emerged from the cloud. Because of him, four other angels came into being from another cloud, and they became attendants for the angelic Self-Generated. The Self-Generated said, 'Let [ ] come into being [ ], and it came into being [ ]. And he [created] the first luminary to reign over him. He said, 'Let angels come into being to serve [him], and myriads without number came into being.

Descending directly from the Absolute, Jesus himself is the Self-Generated One who creates among other things Influence C and higher centers from World 3. [10]   As for Judas, he learns that he is from "that holy generation" of Influence C, the "luminous cloud", destined to become its infamous representative on Earth. Descending directly from the Absolute, Jesus himself is the Self-Generated One who creates among other things Influence C and higher centers.

Inner meanings. Being the thirteenth disciple, however, is not a curse, it is a blessing, an anointment, it is the sacred number twelve, the Amduat, transcending itself to become the first hour of the Book of Day, the morning star of uninterrupted presence, it is Shiva in the role of Tarot Card 13, it is Influence C in the role of Judas playing out the Death Card.

Judas was the only disciple it seems to guess correctly Jesus' transcendent origin, proof positive to Jesus of Judas' own divinity: Judas 15-23: (Speaking to his disciples) Jesus said:

'How do you know me? Truly I say to you, no generation of the people that are among you will know me." When his disciples heard this, they became angry and began "blaspheming against him in their hearts." When Jesus observed their lack of understanding, he said to them, "Why has this agitation led you to anger? Your god who is within you and [...] have provoked you to anger [within] your souls. [Let] anyone of you who is [strong enough] among human beings bring out the perfect human and stand before my face. They all said, 'We have the strength.' But their spirits did not dare to stand before [him] -- except for Judas Iscariot. He was able to stand before him, but he could not look him in the eyes, and he turned his face away, saying: I know who you are and where you have come from. You are from the immortal realm of Barbelo, and I am not worthy to utter the name of the one who has sent you.[11]

What must Judas do that no other disciple has the being to do? In Judas 137 Jesus tells him: "You will exceed all of them. For you will sacrifice the man that clothes me." Here "man that clothes" is a key for the steward completing a sequence of six Work I's, and "me" keys higher centers. "Sacrifice" has a double meaning: its literal meaning, Judas will betray Jesus, and an inner meaning. Judas embodies the sixth step, Long BE, which terminates the sequence and the steward in a wordless state of presence.

At its innermost level of meaning then, the betrayal of Jesus by Judas transcends crime: Thanks to keying, we see that betrayal means the steward "unclothing itself", i.e., getting out of the way so higher centers can appear. It is an integral and necessary part of self-sacrifice in the highest sense.

Returning to the enigmatic passage at the conclusion of Gospel of Judas, could it mean at the inner level that the steward (Judas) ultimately re-enters and fuses with the eternal presence of higher centers (the luminous cloud)? For now at least, we cannot know for certain. For one thing, five lines of text are missing in this passage. For another, even if we had the missing lines, would this make the passage any less a mystery?

VIII. There is a Garden East of Eden...

The allegory. There is a garden east of Eden, longitude 121.3, latitude 39.4, elevation: 1,526 feet, and most of the year under a cloudless blue sky, a bright sun in the day, and beautiful stars at night.

In this garden there are terraced slopes of grapevines, olive groves, and an orchard with groves of plum trees, peaches, orange and lemon trees, and a cemetery nearby. Speckle-winged hawks hover above, looking and diving suddenly for prey. Turkey vultures glide and circle overhead silently on extended wings.

On top of a knoll, overlooking the garden, stands a winery building surrounded by grapevines. Made of 6-inch thick reinforced concrete, unfinished, the building seems abandoned and neglected, but inside there are signs of renewed life.

Years ago, far into the night, machines could be heard crushing raw grapes into wine pulp, pumps could be heard pushing the pulp into stainless steel wine tanks and eventually into wine barrels. And up on the slopes, from dawn 'til sunset, hundreds of men and women could be seen harvesting tons of sweet-smelling grapes.

Now the pumps and machines have been dismantled, the stainless steel tanks torn out of their concrete anchor pads and sold. And those harvesters on the slopes? Only a precious few remain from that generation, but joined now by a younger generation of servants. Inside the winery the tank room looks like Hiroshima after the nuclear explosion. White chalky dust everywhere (from jackhammers ripping thru concrete to remove the tanks.)

In this garden east of Eden cold winters and hot summers are long with lows below freezing and highs above 100 degrees Fahrenheit. Spring and fall are short. Palm trees grow in abundance there and acres of roses sculpted into rose gardens, lotus flowers and avenues of roses and palms.

In this garden there are:

Flowing Italian fountains – Poseidon with a triton mastering two Sea Monsters, the Six Water Nymphs, the Three Graces, the Water Maiden, The Happy Child and -- and Michelangelo's statue of David, intently eying his adversary.

Statues high atop pedestals 30 feet high at the intersections and ends of the avenues of palms and roses. The statues are named after ancient Greek gods and goddesses: Apollo, Eros, Artemis, Athena.

Nurseries for incubating the flowers and palms, and repair shops and wood shops and an art gallery containing collections of paintings, Chinese vases and rare books and a teacher of extraordinary being and virtue tirelessly hosting breakfasts, receptions, dinners and lectures there.

And every day in this garden east of Eden vineyard workers and gardeners work from dawn to sunset in the vineyards, olive groves, orchards and rose and palm gardens and along the avenues of palms and roses. The harvest is abundant, and the laborers are few. Sometimes they can be found incubating and planting young vines, palms and roses in nurseries, and at other times digging up, cutting down and removing to the burn pile plants that have died. There are days -- many days during the long hot summer -- when they are irrigating the plants thru a complex drip irrigation system, with automatic sprinklers and by hand.

There are other days when they are weeding, pruning, trimming, mowing, weed whipping, spraying herbicides, setting gopher traps and fertilizing. And all of this these workers and gardeners do as servants of Influence C, the esoteric school they belong to, and their teacher and spiritual guide, whom they consider a conscious being. The ancient Egyptians called these workers "servants of God", which we moderns loosely translate "servants of

Presence". The ancient Egyptian hieroglyph for these servants gives a more precise meaning: a fuller stick for pounding wet clothes clean, or simply "those who purify".

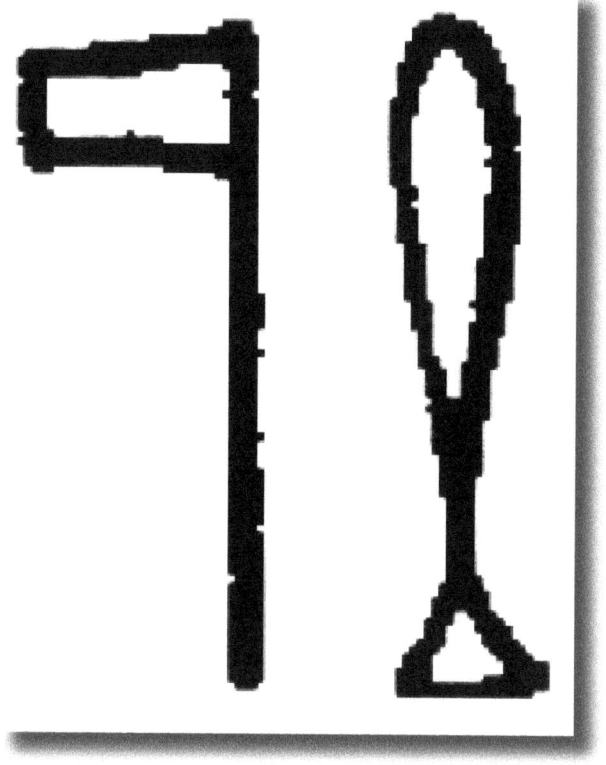

A revelation. One morning something quite strange and wonderful happened to one of these servants. Kneeling down to pull up and remove weeds from around a young palm tree along one of the avenues of roses and palms, he suddenly realized that the keys his teacher and spiritual guide had been teaching him fit this moment of kneeling and pulling perfectly like a key in a familiar lock and, applying it to the moment, unlocked its inner meaning: The young palm tree he was kneeling before in that moment became a metaphor for the Nine of Hearts, the weeds became 10,000 mechanical I's, and he himself kneeling and pulling weeds the steward.

On a higher level, this servant of Presence saw in the young palm a metaphor for himself, a steward serving a higher purpose, and the weeds his King of Clubs generating mechanical I's to keep him pin down to lower instinctive functions.

But if the young palm was a metaphor for the steward, then who was the servant caring for it? For the first time he saw himself through a looking glass: He himself was a living, breathing metaphor for the Higher Self, for the two higher centers, higher emotional and higher intellectual. In a split second two higher plays appeared – keys within keys -- within a third play of quietly living the moment without keys.

The servant of Presence was stunned.

Dark reactions: The Garden of Eden begins inside plant seeds -- of palm, vine, rose, even weeds, all the same -- underground in complete darkness. Plant science teaches us that a series of chemical reactions called dark reactions synthesize high energy molecules and CO_2 into sugar molecules, and these slowly synthesize into tissues made of glucose, starch and cellulose, into chloroplasts and finally into chlorophyll pigment. In the process, the high energy molecules driving these reactions are depleted.

Light reactions. By now the seedlings have been transformed by the dark reactions into young plants, each pushing its way up thru the soil and above ground into the light. In sunlight wave-particles of light striking the surface of the plant are absorbed by the chlorophyll pigments created underground. The energy absorbed knocks electrons in the pigment out of their orbits. This action induces the freeing of electrons from water molecules. The resulting electric current creates more high-energy molecules.

Breathing in and out at the molecular level. The cycle of some high-energy molecules absorbing CO_2 while other high energy molecules reducing them to sugars, starch and cellulose repeats itself, followed by a cycle of chlorophyll pigments absorbing light and inducing an electric current to restore the depleted high energy molecules. Light is being transformed into plant tissue, the plant is growing.

During the life of every plant - fruit trees, vines, palms, lotus plants, rosebushes, weeds - this two-cycle process is being repeated all the time, it is breathing at the molecular level: the inhaling of CO_2 by high energy molecules to create plant tissues and the exhaling of a chlorophyll pigment-induced electric current across a proton gradient to create more high energy molecules.

Inner meaning. Light photosynthesizing into plant tissue is a metaphor. What is its hidden meaning? Higher centers are being transformed into the higher parts of lower centers because of the efforts of these lower parts: Mechanically. Plants do not choose to photosynthesize. There the metaphor ends. Beyond metaphor our own higher centers are being transformed into the Nine of Hearts either intermittently or not at all because we choose to make the effort. Plants do not have a choice, we do. No effort, no transformtion. Intentional effort.

This is a story that begins east of Eden after one has been banished from the Garden of continuous mechanical higher states. It is a story of those of us who have lost our wings and descended into the Amduat to awaken the slumbering Osiris in all of us there.

More hidden meanings. The Winery now deserted on the knoll with its gutted tank room is a metaphor for a broken sequence. But when it was fully operational, itrepresented an apex esoterically in the life cycle of wine production. Harvested from the vines (the harvest representing the completion of six steps in a sequence that began with the pruning and tying of vines in winter), the grapes would pass through a four-step process before arriving in the barrel room: 1) the sorting and separating of healthy, ripe grapes from diseased, overripe and unripe grapes, 2) the crushing of the selected grapes into

wine pulp, 3) the separating of the wine (called May wine after this process) from its pulp using centrifuges, and 4) the adding of yeast to accelerate the fermentation process.

Collectively, this four-step process was considered a metaphor for the transformation of suffering -- in particular, the suffering which comes from crushing Work I's into being (i.e., presence).

Amduat and Book of Day cycles at the subatomic, electronic level. And what about palms, rosebushes and grapevines breathing in and out at the molecular level? The inhaling of CO_2 by high energy molecules is a metaphor for a healing sequence (2-3-1). High energy molecules (matter) enrich CO_2 (form) and transform it into living tissue (life). This happens during dark reactions in the absence of light. Lasting about 12 hours, these reactions represent an Amduat cycle.

The exhaling of electric current, on the other hand, is a metaphor for a regeneration sequence (3-2-1) at the sub-atomic, electronic level. An electric current (form) induced across a hydrogen proton gradient in chlorophyll (matter) re-charges energy-depleted molecules (life). This happens during light reactions. Lasting 12 hours, these reactions represent a Book of Day cycle.[13]

§

We end with a poem from the Odyssey:

> *Once indeed in Delos*
> *I saw something akin to you:*
> *A lovely young palm,*
> *Emerging by*
> *The sacred altar of Apollo....*
> *When I saw that*
> *Unforgettable tree,*
> *I marveled long in my heart,*
> *For never since has there been*
> *Such another of equal beauty*
> *Springing forth from Rhea's*
> *Ancient Earth.*
>
> *August 2009*

GLOSSARY

'When I use a word,' Humpty Dumpty said in rather a scornful tone, 'it means just what I choose it to mean--neither more nor less.'

Lewis Carroll

Be - a one syllable invocation to "be present", meaning "come out of imagination". There are two forms -- Short Be corresponding to the Egyptian hieroglyph un and Long BE corresponding to the hieroglyph au. Coming at the start of a sequence, Short Be pierces the veil

of imagination. Coming at the end, Long BE prolongs the state of presence created by the sequence. Metaphors for Short Be are the Red Crown and Isis. Metaphors for Long BE are the White Crown, Osiris in his mummy state, and the vulture. Short Be's sacred number is one. Long BE's is six.

Book of Day - a companion sacred text to the Amduat. In the same way that the Amduat traces Re's journey through the night (the 2nd state), the Book of Day is tracing Ra's journey through the day from dawn to sunset (the 3rd and 4th states of presence). Unlike the Amduat, instead of having a painting for each hour, the Book of Day depicts all twelve hours in one painting. This means twelve barks of Ra are depicted, and twelve sun disks. Metaphorically, the Book of Day is transcribing higher centers journey from the 3rd state at dawn (Short Be) to the 4th state at noon (Middle Be) back to the 3rd state at sunset (the Long BE of presence).

Written more or less at the same time as the Amduat (15th century BC), the Book of Day employs the same imagery, style and syntax, thus suggesting a common author. The names of nine of the 12 daylight hours are (hours 3,4, and 5 are missing):

1ST HOUR: She Who Lifts Up the Beauty of Ra (SUNRISE)

2nd HOUR: She Who Disperses Darkness

- 3 missing hours --

6th HOUR: The Portal Who Seizes (NOON)

7th HOUR: She Who Gives Joy

8th HOUR: Jubilation

9th HOUR: - described, but unnamed

10th HOUR: She Who Lights the Sky

11th HOUR: Beautiful Sight

12th HOUR: She Who Gives Light in the Island of Life (SUNSET)[14]

broken sequence – Sequences are a special class of ascending octaves. They ascend in order to connect the Nine of Hearts to higher centers. At any point in this ascent sequences may turn into their opposite, they can

"lose their wings" and begin to descend, dragging the steward deeper into imagination. When this happens, the octave is called a broken sequence. Usually this happens at the 4th and 6th steps of a sequence. Since they are ascending, sequences require extraordinary amounts of sex energy. At steps 4 and 6 the energy available for completing a sequence drops off. Why this happens is still unclear. We know that between the 3rd and 4th steps the steward passes thru a mi-fa interval, and again, during the 6th step, when it passes thru a si-do. We know that much, what we do not know is why the sequence slows down in these intervals in the first place.

buffer - a defense mechanism the emotional center creates to protect itself from emotionally traumatic events. Usually in some state of imagination when it creates a buffer, the emo-tional center inserts it between memories of two related emotional events, Like padding between rail car couplers, the defense mechanism is called a buffer because it prevents two contradictory events, often emotionally charged, from colliding and being remembered simultaneously. When remembered together, contradictory memories often cause acute emotional anxiety up to and sometimes including psychotic breaks. The main property of buffers is their invisibility, a person is completely unaware the buffer exists even when his emotional center is using it to "keep up appearances".

centers (of gravity) In the Fourth Lecture of his *Psychology of Man's Possible Evolution*, written in 1934, and the text for a series of lectures attracting thousands in London, Ouspensky presented a schematic box diagram of a man standing sideways to illustrate the principle of the sixfold division of the soul. He called each division a center of gravity or simply a center, one center for intellectual activity, a second for moving or motor-sensory activity, a third for instinctive and a fourth for emotional perceptions. Collectively, he called these the four lower centers and did so to sharply differentiate them from a pair of activities he called higher emotional and higher intellectual centers or simply higher centers. (not shown on the diagram) These higher centers are the seat of revelations, mystical dreams, even mathematical and scientific discoveries.

chief feature - There are 72 divisions of the machine, each representing a negative or positive part of the five lower centers, and manifesting itself as a group of habitually recurring mechanical I's we call features. Among these habitually recurring I's there is one group that dominates and influences the others, this group is called chief feature. Usually tending to too much relativity (tramp) or too little (lunatic feature), chief feature reflects not just one's center of gravity but one's body type and alchemy.

combustion - The higher emotional center (World 12) has to be ignited before there can be presence. The purpose of sequences is to assist the steward do precisely that: ignite higher centers. Starting with Short Be and ending with Long BE and the 4 wordless breaths, this process is called combustion. In a sense, the sequence is the match, higher emotional center the flammable material, and the steward the striker. Red is the color code for combustion.

four wordless breaths - a metaphor for the steward prolonging presence at Long BE and igniting higher emotional center.

Fourth Way. The most recent addition to hermetic teachings, based on the teachings of Georg Gurdjieff and Peter Ouspenski, with roots in Sufi teachings, the *Philakalia*, and ancient Egyptian mystery schools. Fourth Way refers to one of *the four ways*. According to Gurdjieff, these are: 1) *the way of the fakir* based on strengthening the intellectual part of the instinctive-moving center, 2) *the way of the monk* based on strengthening the intellectual part of the emotional center, 3) *the way of the yogi* based on strengthening the intellectual part of the intellectual center, and 4) *the fourth way* based on using the other three ways to balance the intellectual parts of the lower centers. With the aroma of something eclectic, the fourth way is, in fact, a calculated synthesis, a unity designed to be not only greater than the sum of its three parts, but "uncloudy", precise and objective enough to ensnare the hearts and minds of a skeptical, scientifically-trained then 20th-, now 21st-century, audience.

higher centers - Being the seat of presence, the higher emotional and higher intellectual centers are responsible for 3rd and 4th states. Conscience, the emotional perception of truth, self-remembering, the 4 wordless breaths are properties of higher emotions (World 12), Revelations, visionary dreams, interpretation of dreams, prophecies are properties of higher intellectual center (World 6). Their synonym is divine presence, their names the God Within, God, Lord, Third Eye, Eye of Ra, Eye of Horus. Metaphors for higher centers include the sun, the ace of hearts for higher emotions and the ace of diamonds for higher intelligence

hermetic - refers to anything alchemical, magical, or astrological. Hermetic texts are usually subdivided into the philosophical and technical hermetica. The former deals mainly with issues of philosophy, and the latter with magic, potions and alchemy. In The Emerald Tablet, a short work attributed to Hermes Trismegistus, one finds the famous maxim "As above, so below." The actual text of that maxim, as translated by Dennis W. Hauck, is "That which is Below corresponds to that which is Above, and that which is Above corresponds to that which is Below, to accomplish the miracle of the One."

higher self - another name for higher centers, emotionally warm, self-sacrificing, loving, in a state of ecstasy.

imagination - Every 6 seconds an I is born and perishes mechanically inside one of the 72 divisions of our biological machine. Since there are 24 x 60 mins. x 60 seconds in a day, this means there about 24 x 600 = 14,000 I's being born and perishing mechanically each day. About 4,000 of these come and go when we are in first state (In the text, the estimate for mechanical I's in the 2nd state has been rounded to 10,000) This continual cacophony of emotional, intellect-tual and instinctive/moving- centered perceptions jumping into and out of existence like free electrons creates the illusion of a single unified I, of unity and permanence of thought, emotion and feeling. The illusion is called imagination and consists of a continual stream of

I's, one mechanical I coming into existence and wearing the crown of being (an illusion) for six seconds only to be replaced through free association by another mechanical I. A treadmill of mechanical I's without unity, without permanence, without reality. Metaphors for imagination are mountain, water, weeds, sea, clouds, Inferno, Hell, Wheel of Fortune, treadmill.

Influence C – a clinical description for God (higher centers) communicating directly with humanity (the steward and Nine of Hearts) through divine revelation, miracles, divine intervention, wordless shocks, conscious teachers and esoteric schools, past and present. Synonyms: objective memory of humanity, World 6 and World 12. These "influences" are contrasted with B-Influence (sacred texts, sacred art and architecture, lectures, books like this one) documenting Influence C's existence in music, song, poetry, the visual and plastic arts.

The signature of true Influence B is that it always points to Influence C. Influence C and B are both put in sharp contrast to Influence A, representing everything devoted directly or indirectly to perpetuating humanity's biological existence, including the King of Clubs inside each one of us, our biological families, our pursuit of professions, programming of the 72 passions at home and school. Gurdjieff coined the clinical terms A, B, and C-Influence as part of a strategy to make the ancient hermetic teaching more accessible to the West.

inhaling / exhaling 4 wordless breaths - a moving-centered metaphor for the steward prolonging presence at Long BE and igniting higher emotional center. Eight is the sacred number for this state.

intellectual parts of centers - Our biological machines have five lower centers and two higher centers. Each lower center is further divided into three parts -- an intellectual part, an emotional and instinctive parts, with each of these parts being subdivided into negative and positive halves. Intellectual parts of centers refers to the intellectual part of the major division of a center. In terms of Alexander Horn's playing card metaphors, the 10's, 7's, and 4's of each suite, both negative and positive. Other metaphors: men, hands, feet, arms, legs.

Long BE - a one-syllable Work I invoked at the end of a sequence to prolong presence. Metaphors: the White Crown, the vulture, evening star in the West, 4 wordless breaths. Sacred number: 6.

lower centers - The five divisions of our biological machines are: intellectual center, moving center, instinctive center, emotional center and sex center. These are also sometimes called the lower centers in contrast to two other centers: the higher emotional and higher intellectual centers.

lower self - the center of gravity of the five lower centers, the axis around which all the mechanical I's issuing from the five divisions turn. Cold, cal-culating, unemotional, also called the King of Clubs

King of Clubs - a metaphor from a deck of playing cards signifying the intellectual part of the instinctive center, the seat of the biological machine's instinctive intelligence. Synonym: lower self. Its associated metaphors: serpent, Set, Judas, Apopis, hippopotamus, Satan, whale

King of Hearts - a metaphor from a deck of playing cards signifying the seat of the biological machine's emotional intelligence. Its associated metaphor: The White King in chess.

mechanical I - another name for a unit of perception. Based on the velocity of each perception (about one every 6 seconds) there are roughly 14,000 mechanical I's a day, a spinning wheel of emotional, intellectual, instinctive, moving-centered I's jumping into and out of existence like free electrons, creating the illusion of a single unified I. Its metaphor: cackling geese. Whenever a mechanical I promotes negative imagination, devil and demon are appropriate metaphors.

metaphor - a direct comparison between two or more seemingly unrelated subjects that typically uses "is a" or "is the" to join the subjects and open a window of hidden meaning. Thus, the Soul is the King of Hearts, and the King of Hearts is the intellectual part of the emotional center. A metaphor is commonly confused with a simile, which compares two subjects using "like" or "as". An example of a simile: "He was as sly as a fox." Metaphor is direct: "He is a sly fox." Originally, metaphor was a Greek word meaning "to carry or transfer from here to there".

Nine of Clubs – a metaphor from a deck of playing cards for the seat of instinctive intelligence, located in the intellectual part of the instinctive center, responsible for maintaining instinctive homeostasis even at the expense of higher emotional and intellectual states, source of instinctive imagination and 2nd state dreams.

Nine of Hearts - a metaphor from a deck of playing cards for the site of emotional intelligence in the intellectual part of the emotional center, responsible for relativity, scale and emotional discrimination, the seat of the soul called by Ancient Egyptians "the narrow gate" and by Gurdjieff and Ouspensky "the steward". Associated metaphors: boat, house, mansion, temple, earth, palm tree, rosebush, grapevine, lotus flower, carriage, coffin, sarcophagus, burning bush

octave - Originally referring to the eight natural notes in a twelve tone scale having the interesting property that there are two points in the scale when the pitch frequencies slow down -- namely a mi-fa interval between the 3rd and 4th notes and a si-do between the 7th and 8th. Gurdjieff generalized this property into the Law of 7 or Law of Octaves: Everything ascending, without exception, has to first pass through a mi-fa interval and then, if it bridges the interval, through a si-do interval to reach a higher octave of being. Without exception, all the time. The corollary: if one does not bridge the first or second interval, the ascent is broken off, and one descends. One enters a new, descending octave, passing quickly thru its si-do and then descending slowly like Alice in the rabbit hole to a lower mi-fa, only to drop abruptly into the do of a newer, even lower octave of being

presence - 3rd and 4th states of higher centers beyond words. Metaphors: the color blue, a blue sky, sunlight, day.

purification - the process of the steward using a sequence of Work I's to momentarily interrupt the stream of associative mechanical I's in the Nine of Hearts called imagination (see imagination) and create a moment of presence. C

sequence - an octave ascending in 6 steps, and not 8, but retaining all the properties of an 8-note ascending octave: recurrence of steps, movement to higher levels, intervals, the breaking of ascent at the intervals if not enough intelligent efforts are made. Until the 6th step octaves and sequences are identical. But at the 6th step something remarkable happens: The sequence stretches its 6th step to include the last three notes of the octave – A, B, C or LA, SI, DO – plus the si-do interval. That is why this sixth step is called Long BE: it covers a distance at least three times as long as the first step (called Short Be) and on top of that it includes an interval. The si-do interval hidden inside the 6th step is the reason this step is hazardous. (In the Amduat Ancient

Egyptians call this step humorously "Boat That Capsizes") Metaphors for sequence: pyramid, mountain of God, rope, staff, doorway, narrow gate, eye of the needle.

Short Be - a one-syllable Work I invoked at the beginning of a sequence to pierce the veil of imagination, i.e., interrupt the stream of associative, mechanical 6-second I's. Its metaphor: the morning star in the East, the Red Crown combusting. Its sacred number: one.

steward - the Nine of Hearts using its relativity, scale and discrimination to slowly master the lower self and its 72 divisions and place them at the service of higher centers. Starting as an immature emotionally charged magnetic center in search of the meaning of life, the steward finding a school transforms this search into practical work on controlling the lower functions. It becomes Observing I, and then deputy steward able to see the truth, but unable to do anything about it. At a more advanced stage, the steward is mature enough to see things as they are, itself as it is, that it is a nothingness like everything else around it, that the real meaning of life, its crowning achievement, is to live each moment in remembrance of God and Influence C, and simply be present to this.

The steward's methods for reaching this state include using sequences, invoking presence of higher centers directly with Be, Peace, Gods. Its task: to turn the wild hippopotamus inside lower centers into the Bull Without A Halo on Tarot Card 21, to turn the Set inside that tears out Horus Left Eye in the Pyramid Texts into the Set that stands alongside Isis in the 7th Hour of the Amduat using magic to defend Ra from Apopis. Its metaphors: all the historical prophets and heroes of myth: Horus, Joseph, Moses, David, Solomon, Buddha, Jesus, Odysseus, Mohammed, Lao Tze, Arjuna. Animal metaphors: hawk, Anubis, Thoth, dung beetle. The steward is a product of work on oneself in an esoteric school.

Work I - a unit of perception, usually in the intellectual or emotional center and based on the Teaching. Examples of Work I's: "be present", "set noble aims", "Soul", "awaken to the higher reality", "God", "the Soul longs for God", "biological machine", "scale and relativity",

"higher reality", "Nine of Hearts", "King of Clubs", "lower self". Metaphors: 30-foot spear, bows, arrows, sword, whip, garments, stars, grass, grapes, palm leaves.

.

Appendix C Original Sayings of Jesus from the Q Source with Keys for Their Inner Meaning And A Brief Commentary

Jesus said:

I am telling you, love your enemies, bless those who curse you, pray for those who mistreat you.

If someone slaps you on the cheek, offer your other cheek as well. If anyone grabs your coat, let him have your shirt as well.

Give to anyone who asks, and if someone takes away your belongings, do not ask to have them back.

As you want people to treat you, do the same to them.

Don't judge and you won't be judged. For the standard you use will be the same standard used against you.

Can the blind lead the blind? Won't they both fall into a pit?

A student is not better than his teacher. It is enough for a student to be like his teacher.

Keying The Q Source Sayings of Jesus

Jesus said:

I (Higher Centers) *am telling you* (Nine of Hearts), *love* (externally consider, forgive) *your enemies* (the 10,000 mechanical I's of your Lower Self), *bless* (externally consider) *those who curse(express negative emotions) you, pray for* (externally consider) *those who mistreat you* (express negative emotions).

If someone slaps you on the cheek (expresses a negative emotion), *offer your other cheek as well* (externally consider him or her). *If anyone grabs your coat* (expresses a negative emotion), *let him have your shirt as well* (externally consider him or her).

Give to anyone who asks (externally consider him or her*), and if someone takes away your belongings* (expresses a negative emotion), *do not ask to have them back* (externally consider him or her).

As you want people to treat you (externally consider you), *do the same to them* (externally consider them).

Don't judge (don't express a negative emotion)*and you won't be judged* (won't be subjected to a negative emotion). *For the standard you use (externally consider others) will be the same standard used against you* (externally consider others).

Can the blind (a man or women identified) *lead the blind* (a man or women identified)*? Won't they both fall into a pit* (imagination)*?*

A student (a steward making efforts to awaken and succeeding sometimes)*is not better than his teacher* (a conscious being making efforts not to fall asleep and failing sometimes). *It is enough for a student* (a steward awake) *to be like his teacher* (a conscious being awake).

Commentary: Who Was Jesus Really?

Jesus was a Galilean teacher and healer who after the execution of John the Baptist felt it necessary to accelerate and enlarge his mission and finally to bring it to a confrontatory climax in Jerusalem. The teaching had a public and an esoteric element. The Q source, a "sayings" Gospel that we can deduce from its use in later Gospels, indicates a teaching publicly put forward in a peripatetic way throughout Galilee.

Jesus work is curiously similar to the public methods of Socrates and other Greek philosophers. He could, like Socrates, draw a crowd, a fact which made him appear dangerous to the Jewish authorities fearful of the public chaos that would incite Roman brutality. The sayings are tender and beautiful in their simplicity and are rooted in the acceptance and transformation of suffering. Any miracles noted are healings – nothing transgressing the laws of physics, and while there is a shadowy apocalyptic tone, there is nothing of political revolution or any context beyond Judaism and Mosaic Law.

John Craig

APPENDIX D. Plato on the Limits to Metaphor and Allegory

Is there a limit to metaphor? Viewed symbolically, let every atom, molecule and organic part of one level of reality (or cosmos) A_1 be mapped in a one-to-one ratio into every atom, molecule and part of a higher level B_1. Call this mapping reflection and simply represent it as the ratio A_1/B_1.

Now let the mapping of A_1 into B_1 be mirrored at higher levels of reality A_2, A_3, A_4, etc., B_2, B_3, B_4, etc.. and let the operator <-->.represent this mirroring process. How a higher level of reality can mirror a lower (and vice versa) need not concern us for now.

To restate our question in terms of mirrors of reflection, is there a limit to A_1/B_1 <--> A_2/B_2 <--> A_3/B_3 <-->...<-->A_n/B_n, beyond which metaphor collapses into literal-mindedness? If so, that would be the limit to metaphor, there the outer meaning becomes the inner, the inner the outer.

Few in the history of sacred literature have been better qualified to answer this question than Plato. Himself a master of metaphor and allegory, Plato addressed this question in The Republic: "Conceive two levels of reality", he wrote, "One of them the intelligible order, the other the visible... Divide [each level of reality] into two unequal sections." Mathematically, we have two reflections, A_1/B_1, A_2/B_2. An outer visible reality consisting of divisions A_1, B_1, and an inner intelligible order consisting of A_2, B_2.

"In the visible order", Plato observes, " One division consists of images, that is, shadows, reflections in water and on surfaces, the other division will consist of that of which the first division is an image of: animals, plants, man-made objects..." Symbolically, reflection A1/B1. Plato :"Consider the division of the intelligible...there is one section which the soul is compelled to investigate by treating as images things imitated in [the visible world]" A2 " ...while there is another section... in which [the soul] makes no use of images...relying only on ideas..." B2.

In the Phaedrus [Fact check source], thinly veiling himself as a student of Euclid, Plato observes: "[Students of geometry] make use of images and talk about them though they are not thinking of them but of those things of which they are a likeness ...The very things which they mold and draw...these things they treat on their turn as only images, but what they really seek is to get sight of those realities which can only be seen by the mind." Again, symbolically, reflection A2/B2. It would seem for Plato the mirroring of reflections stops two levels deep. A1/B1<-->A2/B2.

Why is that?

Plato explains: At the level of visible reality, "compelled to make assumptions, the soul cannot extricate itself from them to reach first principles. Instead it uses images and likenesses to reach a conclusion...But at the level of intelligible reality consisting of ideas only, the soul uses the dialectic to reason through its assumptions, treating them as hypotheses, underpinnings, springboards, not as absolute beginnings, and in this way it rises to the first principle and starting point of all things and after reaching this it proceeds downward to its conclusion without using images or likenesses."

There is no need to go further than two levels, Plato tells us, because by the end of the first reflection A1/B1 it seems one has exhausted the possibilities of metaphor. There is only the literal meaning of the second reflection in the intelligible order A2/B2 based on dialectical reasoning to first principles.

Not so, observed Rumi some 1500 years later. The truth is there are mirrors within mirrors at least six levels deep. In the Mathnawi Rumi explains cryptically:

Know the words of the Koran are simple, but within the outward sense is an inner secret one. and beneath that secret is a third, dumbfounding the highest wit. Seen by none save God, the Incomparable, the All-Sufficient is the fourth meaning, and thus they go on even to the seventh meaning.[21]

Why is that?

Humanity had to wait another 600 years for a plausible resolution. Through the transparency of Gurdjieff's diagram of cosmoses above and below Organic Life one sees 6 cosmoses extending from the invisible intelligible world of the Absolute (World 3), passing down through the visible worlds of Galaxies, Sun, Planets (Worlds 6, 12, and 24) above Organic Life to the imaginary world of the Moon (World 96) below. Each cosmos is a mirror of reflections in the cosmos immediately above and below it.

This mirroring recurs six times. Only four concern us here: The efforts of the steward to escape imagination and be present (Moon) is a metaphor mirroring presence of higher centers (Sun) which in turn mirrors presence of C-Influence (Galaxies), and beyond this, presence of the Absolute transcending metaphor and shattering its mirror. Gurdjieff's solution: The number of levels coincides with the number of cosmoses minus 1 which is six levels (including the shattered mirror for transcendence).

IMAGE CREDITS

Cover photo: Camel at Sunset; Amduat images from Tomb of Thuthmosis III, Valley of the Kings; Ceiling Mosaics of Creation and Expulsion from the Garden, Michaelangelo, Vatican; The Charioteer, Delphi Museum, Greece; Gustav Dore, illustrations for Dante's Divine Comedy; Heiroynimus Bosch, Souls Ascending into Light; Rembrandt, Etchings of Christ Teaching; Gurdjieff, Ray of Creation, in Ouspensky, In Search of the Miraculous; Leonardo Da Vinci, the Last Supper; Palms, roses and vineyard photos by the Fellowship of Friends.

END NOTES

1 Graham Hancock, *The Supernatural*

2 Zeus: "Hera, come lie down, and let us enjoy the delights of love" in Kostas Papaioannou, *The Art of Greece*,(N.Y., 1989) pp. 57-58.

3 Brooks Haxton, *Fragments: The Collected Wisdom of Heracleitus* (NY, 2001), pg. 89

4 Plato, *Republic, Bk III*, 390.b

5 Shortly after the execution of Socrates, it is reported that Plato set out on a journey of mourning for his teacher and friend lasting several years. His travels may have taken him to Egypt where he studied at the temples of Karnak and Luxor.

6 A more radical reading is that the Higher Self, higher centers are "seeing" is none other than the Absolute.

7 *Satyagraha* is a form of resistance developed by Mohandas Karamchand Gandhi—popularly known as Mahatma Gandhi—which emphasizes the search for truth and attempts to change the heart as well as the actions of the opponent. The word literally means "with the force of love and truth".

8 *Gospel According to Thomas* (Leiden, 1959)

9 *The Gospel of Judas verses 142-144* (National Geographic, 2006)

10 See *Judas 86-99* for the revelation.

11 In Sethian gnostic texts, Barbelo is the Divine Mother of All, Forethought (pronoia) of the Absolute. The name itself is a form of the Hebrew four-letter word for God (YHWH) meaning "God (b-)-in-four (arb(a)"

12 Rodney Collin, *idem.*, pp. 189-203

13 See Glossary entry for Book of Day.

14 Original ful text of *Book of Day* (based on Alexander Piankoff's translation):

First Hour: "The majesty of this God [Re] comes forth from the Hour whose name is She Who Lifts Up the Beauty of Re. This is the Hour of Appeasement... He appears in the land of the inhabitants of the horizon.

Beautiful navigation to make all men, all cattle, all worms, everything he has created live. She rises before Truth."

Second Hour: "The majesty of this God travels in the Hour whose name is She Who Disperses Darkness. This is the Hour of Triumph. It is the Second Hour of the day and the one in which the majesty of this god comes out. His is the Hour of Jubilation and Adoration of Re when he comes out of her. She rises before Will."

-- Text for 3rd, 4th and 5th Hours Missing--

Sixth Hour: "The majesty of this God goes toward the Hour whose name is the Portal Who Seizes. This Hour is the sixth Hour of the day. Rise, rise, let the gods who are in the bark rise in order to repulse Apopis. Let Seth stretch forth his arm to let Apopis fall! – says Isis in her incantation. She rises before Seth."

Seventh Hour: "The voyage of the majesty of this God on the sand bank toward the Hour named She Who Gives Joy, toward this Hour which is the Seventh of the day. The gods in the great bark, their hearts are joyful after the journey. She rises before Horus."

Eighth Hour: "Passage made by the God over the sand bank toward the Hour called Jubilation. This Hour is the Eighth Hour of the day...the gods who are in [the bark] are in jubilation when Apopis is overthrown and when his majesty is justified. She rises before Khonsu."

Ninth Hour: "This Hour is the Ninth Hour of the day, and the one in which the passage toward the Yaru fields is made while the gods who are in the bark navigate it. She rises before Isis. All the gods come out in great jubilation owing to its greatness, the sky is in beauty, the earth is in peace. These gods take hold of the Nefert-rope, the one which is in the bark. The hearts of the gods in their shrines are in joy, they grant life. Atum, after having passed the sand bank, will overthrow the enemies of Re."

Tenth Hour: "Navigating in peace inside the Tenth Hour, She Who Lights the Sky, who refreshes the oars. It is the Hour to descend in the Bark of the Evening for the crossing in the West. She rises before Magic, the Elder."

Eleventh Hour: "Navigating in peace in the Eleventh Hour whose name is Beautiful Sight. It is the Hour of adjusting the ropes toward the Western

Horizon when the boat goes down from the West. She rises before He Who Adjusts The Ropes which are in the boat."

Twelfth Hour: "Navigating in peace in the Twelfth Hour whose name is She Who Gives Light in the Island of Life. It is the hour when this God [Re] rests in life in the West and gives offerings, takes care, makes...She rises for the One Who Protects in the twilight."

15   K. Khosla, *The Sufism of Rumi* (Element Books, 1987), p. 21

16   K. Khosla, p. 22

17   K. Khosla, p. 22 – 25

18 K. Khosla, p. 179-180.

19 Source: Clark@Libertypages

20 The 10 emanations are:

Keter Elyon - the highest point above, the crown, the divine Will, the "I am"

Hokhmah - wisdom, hidden thought, primeval being, father, YHWH (upper)

Binah - understanding or intelligence, repentance, palace, mother, Eloheim (upper) Hesed - love, greatness, goodness, light

Gevurah (din) - power, judgment, fear, wrath, strength, darkness

Tiferet - beauty, mercy, firmanent, YHWH (lower), Sun

Nezah - eternity or endurance

Hod - majesty

Yesod - foundation

Malkhut - kingdom or sovereignty, Israel, supernal earth

shekhinah (divine presence)

Eloheim (lower), Moon

Source: Clark@Libertypages

21 Rumi, *The Masnavi* (trrans. E.H. Whinfield, Octagon Press, London, 1979), pg. 169

Book 3: It Happened on the Way From Africa: The Origin and Meaning of Hieroglyphs
2012

Ascend, I follow thee, safe Guide.
John Milton

3/23/2012 5:50 PM **Our miraculous story** will be woven together out of three separate, seemly unrelated strands of evidence: 1) the evidence from Gardiner's hieroglyphic sign list [1] suggesting layers of meaning spanning perhaps tens of thousands of years; 2) the depiction of South African San dancers some 30,000 years ago in positions almost identical to those of Ancient Egyptian dancers depicted in temples dedicated to Hathor; 3) the enigmatic hieroglyph for God matching an image on a prehistoric cave painting in Spain some 15,000 to 20,000 years old. These three pieces may have in common a single extraordinary property – trance states induced it seems by the hallucinogenic molecule DMT (dimethyltrytamine).

Trance states: the theory. In the 1988 issue of *Current Anthropology* neuro-psychologist David Lewis-Williams advanced the theory that pre-historic cave paintings were in fact recordings of shaman priests entering trance states and hallucinating encounters with beings of another dimension. To test his hypothesis Lewis-Williams ap- plied it to the prehistoric rock paint-ings of the ancient San culture in South Africa and to the roc art of the Native American Shoshonean Coso culture of the California Basin. To make the necessary correlations with the neuro-psychological states of living subjects, Lewis-Williams triangulated the pattern of rock art using paintings drawn by living LSD patients.

---

1   Alan Gardiner, *Egyptian Grammar* (Griffith Institute, 3rd edition, 1957)

The results were astonishing: In each test the rock art images fell into the same sequence of six trance state patterns documented for the LSD patients. Lewis-Williams christened these patterns *entoptic phenomena*. Invited numerous times to test the theory on himself, Prof. Lewis-Williams declined.

The six patterns Lewis-Williams documented:

Pattern I: grids, lattices, and expanding hexagons
Pattern II: sets of parallel lines
Pattern III: dots, flecks, tiny circles
Pattern IV: angular, sometimes undulating zigzag lines
Pattern V: nested catenary curves
Pattern VI: filagrees, thin meandering lines

LSD patients reported the patterns being dynamic, energetic, ever-changing "incandescent, shimmering, moving, rotating" and sometimes expanding. (Lewis-Williams & Dowson, 'The Signs of All Times', *Current Anthropology*, vol. 29, 203-205)

The stages of altered consciousness Lewis-Williams and his colleague Dowson observed and documented are as interesting as the six patterns. Reviewing field reports on patients administered hallucinogenic drugs over several decades, Lewis-Wiliams and Dowson concluded that patients experiencing the pattern of six shapes normally progressed through three altered states of consciousness:

Stage I: Only entoptic phenomena

Stage II: Observer re-ordering the entoptics into icons (snakes, animals, etc.)

Stage III: Full-scale hallucinations of animals, men, women, some half-animal, some half-men

Trance states: the practice. In his 2006 study *Supernatural* Graham Hancock turned Lewis-William's 3-stage 6-pattern model on its head. Applying it to two more cultures -- the artists of Upper Paleolithic paintings and the artists of Ancient Egyptian wall carvings and papyri (Hancock, 205-209, 544-552) --, Hancock made similar confirmations:

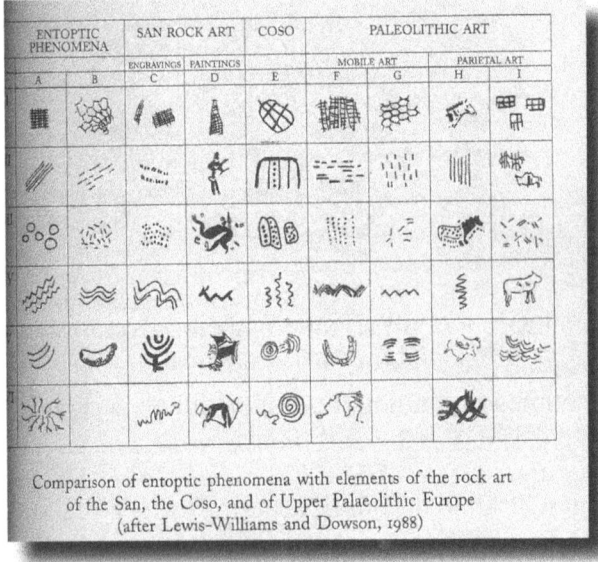

Comparison of entoptic phenomena with elements of the rock art of the San, the Coso, and of Upper Palaeolithic Europe (after Lewis-Williams and Dowson, 1988)

Only this time the interpretation would be paradigm-shattering. Schrodinger's cat was out the bag:

For thousands of years shaman priests had been riding the DMT molecule like a 3-stage booster rocket to dial into *a parallel dimension that actually exists* alongside our normal 4-dimensional spacetime. In trance states induced by ingesting the ayahuasca and similar plants containing DMT, Hancock argued, these men and women had been entering a parallel dimension, meeting beings of extraordinary intelligence and compassion there and receiving spiritual and even technological guidance from them. This parallel dimension and the beings inhabiting it -- not hallucinations -- were, and still are, the potent source of humanity's recorded wisdom and knowledge. True to his craft, Hancock began experimenting extensively with DMT *on himself* to verify his discovery. To say the least, the scientific community is up in arms, it will never be the same. The Tobacco, Drug and Firearms Department is keeping a close eye on Mr. Hancock.

Ancient Egyptian hieroglyphs: a cold case. In the case of Ancient Egyptian culture, while recording the most obvious connections in funerary wall paintings of ram-headed Ra, hawk-headed Horus, Anubis the Jackal and Seth the strange sleek-headed Dog, Hancock missed the rich vein of further confirmations hidden openly in Egyptian hieroglyphs themselves.

Using Gardiner's sign list to extend Hancock's entoptic phenomena table to Egyptian hieroglyphs, we see in Table B the following:

1) Five of the six entoptic patterns discovered by Lewis-Williams and confirmed by Hancock were also uncovered in our cursory inspection, suggesting not simply coincidence but *parentage.* If not the mother, leaving no doubt, then the San culture of South Af-

rican is more than likely the genetic father of ancient Egyptian hieroglyphs, and if not that, most definitely its next of kin (sibling, uncle or aunt).

2) Sixteen of the twenty hieroglyphs from the early period (8,000 BC to 3,000 BC) are matched by San rock paintings dating back to 15,000 BC to 20,000 BC. Eleven of 60 hieroglyphs from the middle period (3500 to 1500BC) represent combinations of those sixteen. In all, 27 hieroglyphs (nearly 40 percent) of the 75 hieroglyphs studied here closely resemble San images.

Suggestive at best, these startling discoveries *do not* constitute a proof that ancient Egyptian priests were, in fact, shamans using hallucinogenic plants to enter and exit a parallel dimension. They simply remind us that *this possibility cannot be ruled out*[2]

3/26/2012 8:30 PM. At the end of the day though, what does this all mean? For certain, the approach offered by Lewis-Williams and Hancock is quite stunning. To discover correlations between the observations of LSD patients entering and exiting trance states today and records left behind thousands of years ago in rock art, funerary paintings and ancient hieroglyphs is paradigm-shattering. But after the hoopala and dust settles, the missing link is still missing: the meaning of the original communication. Messages left behind thousands of years ago to perhaps remind us of altered states of consciousness -- are still maintaining their "majestic silence".[3]

---

2   In principle, no amount of triangulation can ever lead to a complete proof unless experimenters with hallucinogenic herbs or LSD start reporting visits with half-animals/half-men speaking ancient Egyptian.

3   Plato, *Phaedrus*, 275e

Is then the layer of meaning connecting the evidence of altered states thousands of years ago with their original meaning lost forever?

Like a cold case murder mystery, we have only one clue: a tiny strand of esoteric DNA left behind which may or may not solve the mystery. The strand: In *Phaedrus* Plato relates the myth of an Egyptian pharaoh named Ammon who chastised one of his own gods Thoth for inventing hieroglyphs. Inventor of mathematics, geometry and astronomy, Thoth proudly boasted to Ammon that his invention would "make the people of Egypt wiser and improve their memory. [Hieroglyphs] provide a recipe for memory and wisdom", the god said. [4]

Ammon observed sadly:

> Because of your fondness for hieroglyphs you have stated the very opposite of its true effect. If we men learn this, it will implant forgetfulness in our souls, we will cease to exercise memory because we rely on written hieroglyphs, *calling things to remembrance no longer from within, but by means of external marks* [5].

A solution:

A) Rock art of the San culture (and inside Lascaux and Chauvet), paintings inside the tombs of Tuthmosis, Ramses VI and inside coffins and on papyri, the temple wall carvings at Karnak, Luxor and hieroglyphs and other forms of divinely inspired writing all have one purpose: *To remind those who already know their meaning what they meant*.) By themselves they cannot instruct or teach anyone else anything. One has

---

4   Plato, *Phaedrus*, 274e
5   Plato, *Phaedrus*, 275b

to be very simple-minded and naïve," Socrates observes, "if he believes hieroglyphs or any other form of writing can do anything more than *remind one who already knows.*"[6]

Hieroglyphs define the limits of our ordinary logical states of perception and thinking. *The knowledge required to decode them transcends these limits,* coming as it does perhaps from the higher dimension shaman priests enter and exit from (aka a higher mind), and not from the hieroglyphs and paintings themselves. That is why, without someone who already has this higher knowledge recovering the original meaning and instructing the rest of us, hieroglyphs, paintings and rock art are pure nonsense, a source of mischief and pointless suffering. Like two streams – one of a higher objective reality, the other of knowledge and understanding of it -- flowing parallel to one another, the stream of an ancient teaching flows along invisibly and inconspicuously next to the stream of material artifacts attracting tens of thousands of tourists as *the higher knowledge of their meaning.* This stream is not lost, it's just *hidden and minding its own business.*

Without a guide or teacher *who already has this higher knowledge,* images, hieroglyphs and other forms of writing simply create in us *a momentary illusion of learning and knowing* something. Like cotton candy nothing sticks. A practical question: Where does one find such guides? Typically eccentric individuals, these men and women are usually not to be found simply walking the streets bare-headed nor locked up in universities. The main purpose of esoteric schools of the kind Buddha, Christ, Lao Tzu, Rumi, Gurdjieff and others organized is to shelter and protect men and women with this higher knowledge, permitting them to live out their lives safely and instruct the rest of us. That tradition continues.

---

6   Plato, *Phaedrus*, 275d

4/02/2012 8:44 AM. *God has no hieroglyph.* Stripped of vowels, and reduced to the consonants *ntr,* the hieroglyph for God is both revealing and puzzling. The transliteration has several meanings: 1) "that which is", 2) "that which binds or knits together", and 3) "sacred anointing stream ". The puzzling part is the meaning to attach to the images themselves --sometimes simply a flag by itself, sometimes a hawk on a pedestal, sometimes both. At other times, a bearded man or a phallus (presumably designating a male divinity), at other times a seated woman or a cobra (presumably for a female divinity), and sometimes vultures. Are these really hieroglyphs for God?

The images share one interesting property: *None of them has any known phonetic value,* which means it is not possible to dismiss them simply as carriers of sound without any intrinsic meaning. And there the mystery deepens.

Assuming the alleged hieroglyphs for God have an intrinsic meaning and are revealing something about God, what could that possibly be? We have several choices: 1) admit we don't know and move on, 2) engage in the kind of haphazard guesswork one often encounters in well-meaning scholars who really don't know (see Redford or Medler for examples), or 3) consider the hieroglyphs in the light of Graham Hancock's intriguing thesis: that Egyptian priests were, in fact, ancient shamans experiencing hallucinogenic states of altered consciousness much as modern shamans do.

If true, in these states the hieroglyphs for Ra, Isis, Osiris, Seth, and the other Egyptian divinities represent precisely what the ancient Egyptian shamans saw, neither more nor less. They are not symbols of reality with some hidden inner meaning. In some mysterious sense they *are* reality, i.e., a transcript of a higher dimensional world Egyptian shamans visited, "saw" and recorded repeatedly (Hancock, *The Supernatural*).

Having said this much, one opens the door a little to controversy. Are these non-phonetic images for God --flag, hawk, phallus, bearded man, etc. -- *really* telling us something about the ancient Egyptian vision of his/her/its divine presence? Or are they transmitting a different message entirely? For more than a half century the door to this question was effectively locked by a generation of Egyptologists who ridiculed anyone daring to ask. Referred to knowingly as the "image trap", generations of students were (and still are) cautioned to steer clear of reading anything into those enigmatic images. And yet sooner or later one must "read something into them" to avoid the flip side of image traps, namely the phonetic trap, i.e. refusing to interpret any non-phonetic image which cannot be understood in the conventional way (by context, usage, etc.).

Returning to our question: A flag presumably extending from a flagpole, what could this mean? Or stated differently what were the Egyptian shamans recording? Evidence from the Sabossona prehistoric caves near Vichi, France circa 25,000 BC suggest that flags may have been a recurrent part of the shaman vision. There we find a flag extending from a dotted circle – the flag bearing an uncanny resemblance to the hieroglyph for God, the dotted circle resembling the hieroglyph for the sun.

Separated in time by tens of thousands of years and in space by several thousand kilometers, what does *this* flag image have in common with the Egyptian hieroglyph? A strong wind. Seriously. Neither flag is limp, and not because the artists knew nothing about limp flags or how to draw them. It was their intention to illustrate thru the image of a flag extended erectly from a flagpole the visible effect of the unseen, the imperceptible, the invisible --the wind itself, Divine Presence.

Flag, then, may be a key for "being in the Presence of God", but it is definitely *not* a symbol for God itself. *There is no symbol for this.* Likewise with the other non-phonetic hieroglyphs for God, they are all keys for the effects of divinity, and not divinity itself: keenness of vision, telescopic vision, fearlessness and ferocity (the falcon), intelligence and virility (the bearded man, the sperm-dripping phallus), tenderness, fertility and motherly love (the seated woman, the vulture), but *no hieroglyph for the Divinity itself.*

4/02/2012 11:16 AM. *Hathor fertility dancing.* On the way to his paradigm-shattering discovery of a presumably universal pattern to altered states of shaman consciousness *transcending space and time* David Lewis-Williams reported on the Ju-ho-ansi trance dance depicted frequently on San rock paintings in the Drakensberg area. Puzzled by paintings thousands of years old which show human figures bent forward at the waist with their arms stretched out behind their backs, Lewis-Williams observed, "no ethnographer [of San people] of the 19th or 20th century seems to have recorded this posture" (Hancock, 187) Then in 1975, while traveling through the Kalahari Desert with American anthropologist Megan Biesele, Lewis-Williams watched in astonishment as a San shaman stood up and began bending slightly forward with his arms behind him. Through Biesele the interpreter, the shaman explained: This was how "shamans danced when they were asking God to put more potency in their bodies." (Ibid)

Imagine the present author's own surprise in 2011 when he opened Alison Robert's delightful study[7] to a photo from the tomb of Kheruef at Thebes showing young female dancers with long braided hair bent forward with arms behind them performing fertility dances at the Sed Festival of Amenhotep III (1386-1349BC), father of Akhenaten. Two panels -- one showing the arms behind, the other showing them forward -- suggest the dancers were moving rhythmically, now forward, now back, now forward again twisting their bodies hypnotically as they moved (Roberts, 26-27). This discovery confirms again the close, perhaps parental connection between the South African San culture, tens of thousands of years old, and the Ancient Egyptian civilization of North Africa.

For all the novelty, none of these discoveries and new connections are surprising. Core samples of oxygen-isotopes suggest global warming cycles triggered two waves of modern

---

7   A. Robert, *Hathor Rising: The Power of the Goddess in Ancient Egypt* (Inner Traditions International, 1997)

human migration out of Africa. The first following a period of devastating droughts and a genetic bottleneck that nearly wiped out the human species (130,000 BC +/- 21,000 years), the second migration happening around 45,000 BC +/- 21,000 years leading to fierce often violent competition between modern humans and their Neanderthal cousins in Europe and to the extinction of the latter.[8] (The +/- 21,000 year variance accounts for the combined effects of precession, tilt and the Earth's elliptical orbital motion on global climate changes which triggered the migrations in the first place.[9])

In both the first and second migrations the paths were similar: Out of South Africa, through the Nile Valley, then fanning out through the Middle East, Greece, India, China and Europe. The implication: We are tracing out not just the movement of humans and livestock over tens of thousands of years, but the evolutionary path of human civilization as well. The high correlation between San rock art and Egyptian hieroglyphs and the similar coincidence of dancers on San rock art and dancers carved on the walls of Kheruef's tomb are just two visible tips of an immense iceberg of hidden connections.

B) Looking back at the origin and meaning of hieroglyphs

---

8   According to mitochondrial timing techniques, modern humans migrated from Africa during the middle Paleolithic era (352,000-130,000 BC), spreading over the ice-free world during the late Pleistocene. Humans in this migration interbred with archaic human forms already outside of Africa by the late Pleistocene, incorporating archaic human genetic material into the modern human gene pool. See: http://en.wikipedia.org/wiki/Pleistocene. For evidence of a 2nd migration circa 45,000 BC read Stephen S. Hall, "Last of the Neanderthals: Why Did Our Ice Age Rivals Vanish?" *National Geographic*, Oct 2008, vol. 214 and Peter Kessler, *Prehistoric World Hominid Chronology* (26 July 2005. Updated 1 April 2012) http://www.historyfiles.co.uk/ FeaturesAfrica/HominidChronology7.htm

9   See http://en.wikipedia.org/wiki/Milankovitch_cycles

from our new vantage point, Plato's story of Ammon meeting with the Egyptian god Thoth takes on added significance: It is not *just* a myth, it could be a transcript of an altered state of consciousness of shaman priests meeting conscious beings living in a dimension parallel to ours and instructing us directly on occasion. Either handed down by oral transmission from the ancient Egyptians to their Greek disciples until it reached Plato who transcribed it or experienced directly by Socrates and Plato, the Myth of Ammon and Thoth joins others documented throughout Plato's dialogues: the Myth of Er, the Myth of the Cave, the Myth of the Winged Charioteer, etc. – all representing perhaps transcripts of altered states of consciousness.

C) Our one strand of esoteric DNA from Plato's *Phaedrus* seems to have yielded a lot. It carries the strongest implications to date suggesting not just San South African roots for hieroglyphs, but also the branching out of the esoteric school of the Ancient Egyptians into Greece, Persia and

newcomers may have combined to push Neanderthals into a few outposts before they went extinct.

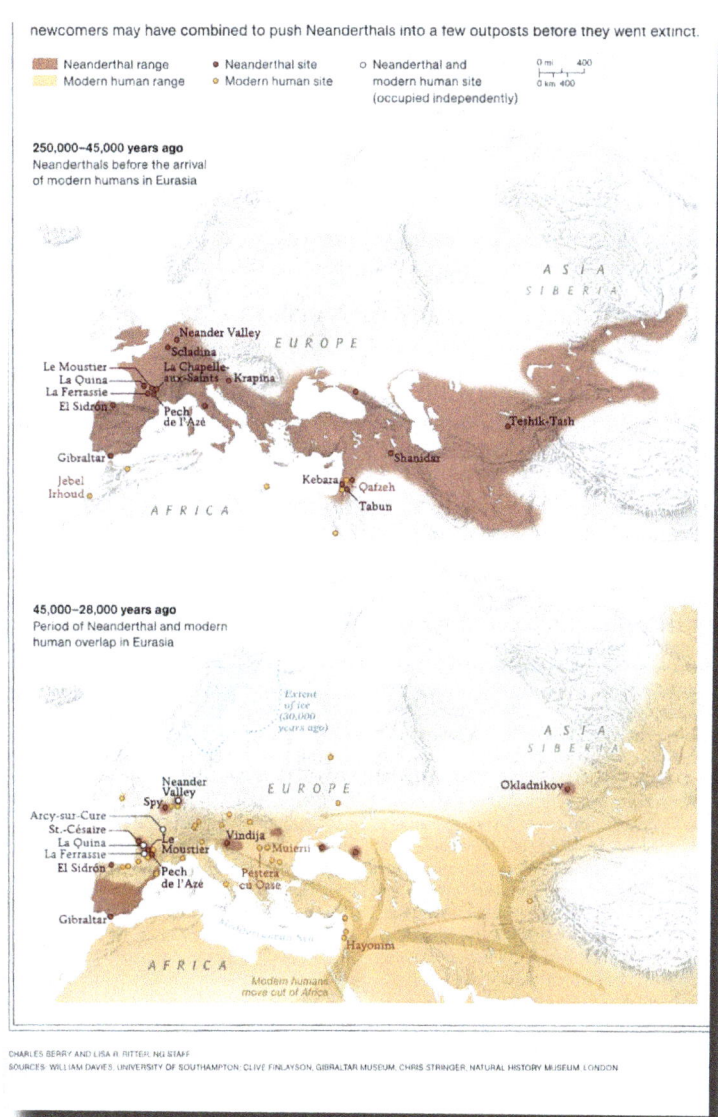

Neanderthal range
Modern human range
● Neanderthal site
○ Modern human site
○ Neanderthal and
    modern human site
    (occupied independently)

250,000–45,000 years ago
Neanderthals before the arrival
of modern humans in Eurasia

ASIA
SIBERIA

Neander Valley
EUROPE
Scladina
Le Moustier
La Chapelle-
aux-Saints Krapina
La Quina
La Ferrassie
El Sidrón
Pech
de l'Azé
Teshik-Tash
Gibraltar
Shanidar
Jebel
Irhoud
Kebara Qafzeh
AFRICA
Tabun

45,000–28,000 years ago
Period of Neanderthal and modern
human overlap in Eurasia

Extent
of ice
(30,000
years ago)

ASIA
SIBERIA

Neander
Valley EUROPE Okladnikov
Spy
Arcy-sur-Cure
St.-Césaire
La Quina Le Vindija
La Ferrassie Moustier Muierii
El Sidrón
Pech
de l'Azé Peștera
cu Oase
Gibraltar
Hayonim
AFRICA
Modern humans
move out of Africa

CHARLES BERRY AND LISA R. RITTER, NG STAFF
SOURCES: WILLIAM DAVIES, UNIVERSITY OF SOUTHAMPTON; CLIVE FINLAYSON, GIBRALTAR MUSEUM; CHRIS STRINGER, NATURAL HISTORY MUSEUM, LONDON

Turkey and its continuation there after disappearing in Egypt. And finally this: *Plato may have been a shaman priest, and Socrates most definitely.* (Plutarch and the oracles at Delphi and Dodona for certain)[10].

3/31/2012 1:58 PM Do the Ancient Egyptian hieroglyphs have a layer of meaning still hidden from view -- undisclosed by the Standard Model and unearthed providentially by the Hancock/ Lewis-William's shaman-entoptic phenomena studies? Short answer: One has to do more than inspect Gardiner's sign lists to find out. Four funerary texts, representing texts with a clear sacred purpose, are available for this purpose: *The Pyramid Texts, the Amduat, Going forth By Day (aka the Egyptian Book of the Dead) and the Book of The Two Ways.* Suppose though one makes the effort and reaches that level, what then? Remembering Plato's rule of thumb, if there's no guide who already knows -- either directly or by oral transmission --, then the effort is an exercise in futility. Even if by some lucky guess one were to stumble upon the deeper layer of meaning, without a (shaman) guide it would be like stumbling into a dark cave without a flashlight. We address this issue in our next volume and offer a solution, if not a flashlight.

GM 4/07/2012

---

10   Roger Lipsey, *Have You Been to Delphi?* (State University of N.Y. Press, 2001)

Book 4: The Mysterious Origin And Strange Descent of Chess: The Path of Evolutionary Inventive Drift
2015

For some minutes Alice stood without speaking, looking out in all directions over the country--and a most curious country it was. There were a number of tiny little brooks running straight across it from side to side, and the ground between was divided up into squares by a number of little green hedges, that reached from green hedges, that reached from brook to brook.

I declare it's marked out just like a large chessboard!' Alice said at last. 'There ought to be some men moving about somewhere --and so there are!' She added in a tone of delight, and her heart began to beat quick with excitement as she went on. 'It's a great huge game of chess that's being played--all over the world--if this IS the world at all, you know. Oh, what fun it is! How I WISH I was one of them! I wouldn't mind being a Pawn, if only I might join--though of course I should LIKE to be a Queen, best.'

Lewis Carroll,
Through the Looking Glass

God always remains a mystery.
Philokalia

*A Senet game painted on the wall
of the tomb of Egyptian Queen Nefertari
(1295–1255 BC)*

Some Humbling Facts. We do not know who invented chess any more than we know for sure when or where it was invented. But that has not prevented no less than seven contending origin theories from surfacing in recent years: Five claiming Chinese origins, one an African-Egyptian origin, and one a Persian-Indian origin.

A Chinese origin?   In his 1997 paper *Facts on the Origin of Chinese Chess (Xiangqi)*[1] Peter Banaschak cast the net of probable origins for chess wide, netting no less than five suspect hypotheses. He writes:

> In the elder Chinese literature five hypotheses on the origins of Chinese Chess feature prominently The list follows Zhou Jiasen and Li Songfu. Ordered according to the antiquity they ascribe to Chinese Chess these hypotheses are :

---

1   http://history.chess.free.fr/papers/Banaschak%201997.pdf

1. An origin in the age of the legendary Shennong (trad. reigned 2737-2697 BC), as proposed by the Yuan (1206-1368) monk Nianchang (1282-1342?) "In olden times Shennong used the sun (ri), the moon (yu),the stars (xing), and the planets (chen) as symbols (xiang); the Tang Minister of State Niu Sengru used chariots (che), horses (ma), scholars (shi), soldiers(zu), and catapults (pao) to replace these as utensils in the game."

2. An origin in the age of the legendary Huangdi (trad. reigned 2697-2597 BC), the Yellow emperor, as proposed by Zhao Buzhi (1053-1110) of the Beisong (Northern Song, 960-1126) in his 'Rules for wide Xiangqi: Foreword "Xiangxi is a game of strategy; Huangdi in his wars used fierce animals in his battle array; as Elephants (xiang) are the strongest of wild animals, the game is called Xiangxi after this strategy." ... Xiangxi was thus ascribed an origin in the third millennium BC, if we place these cultural heroes before the first dynasty.

3. An origin in the age of Zhou (1122-249 BC) Wuwang (reigned1122-1115 BC), in the time of this last campaigns against the tyrant Shang Zhou (reigned 1154-1122 BC), as proposed by Ming (1368-1644) time Xie Zaihang (=Xie Zhaozhe, 1567- 1624) in his "Wuzazu ('Investigations on the five categories of things')" , thus ascribing Chinese Chess an origin in the late 12th century BC. Xiangqi, according to tradition made by King Wu of Zhou in the time of his final campaigns against Shang; if that is not so, at least it became popular among military personnel in the time of the contending realms, as in this time chariot warfare was still important."

4. An origin in the time of the contending realms (475-221 BC). This was proposed in Hu Yinglin's (1551-1602) Bicong ('Brush notes', a kind of essays) , and the "Qianqueju leishu ('Encyclopaedia of hidden and real conditions')" , which was compiled by Chen Renxi(1581-1636), thus ascribing Xiangqi an origin in the third century BC, "Yong Menzhousaid to Mengchangjun: My lord, if you are at leisure, play Xiangqi; thus it was a thing from the time of the contending realms. Because in the strategy of the contending realms the people of this time used elephants just as in the board game strategy (qishi)." The prince Mengchang mentioned here was a well-known man who lived during the times of the last Zhou-king; thus the admonition quoted here would point to a date in the late third century BC.

5. An origin in the time of Beizhou (Northern Zhou, 557-589)Wudi(reigned 561-578), as proposed in the "Taiping yulan ('Grand mirror of the Taiping era')" (completed in 982) under the heading 'Xiangqi. "Zhou Wudi created Xiangxi", the "Wuyuan ('Source of Things')" of Ming Meng Qi explains: "Zhou Wudi made Xiangqi".

Banaschak's Choice. Banaschak's argument is quite impressive, but his critical apparatus is flawed. Having cast his net wide, he does something very strange and un-Sherlock Holmes-like. He narrows down the range for the most probable true origin too quickly. In this case, to hypothesis 4. And on what grounds? That the internal consistency supporting hypotheses 1 through 3 is much weaker, ranging from mythology in the case of hypotheses 1 to historically-based, but less internally consistent hypotheses 2 and 3. Compelling, but unconvincing.

The flaw in Banaschak's argument is that it is one-dimensional. It does not allow for random evolutionary drift of forms over time -- in this case, of chess piece imagery and chess rules. His dismissive attitude toward hypothesis 1 is both symptomatic of this and revealing.[2] Why are "explanations and reasons offered [for hypothesis 1] of such secondary nature that they bear no real value." If nothing else, to its credit, mythology or not, hypothesis 1 is alluding to a mutation and paradigm shift in chess game form on a planetary scale -- from a chess game based on astronomy and divination to one based on strategic military thinking -- a seismic earthquake event that may have happened thousands of years ago.

Interestingly enough, from a completely independent source, Lao Tzu confirms this event.[3] Contrary to Banaschak's dismissive attitude, if it happened at all, this shift has tremendous "real value". Is it possible then there was a chess prototype based on star-mapping? Purpose? *To keep its players mentally sharp and alert for divinations based on direct observation of the movements of the Sun, Moon, stars and planets.* If so, where? Africa.

A mancala origin. Every good detective story begins with a list of the most likely suspects – plus one. The "plus one" is the suspect you would have never imagined. At some opportune

---

2   http://history.chess.free.fr/papers/Banaschak%201997.pdf, p. 6

3   Hua Ching Ni, *The Later Teachings of Lao Tzu*, p. 49

point in the story the author wants you to piece together for yourself who done it, without ever naming names. From bits and pierces of evidence he leaves randomly at the scene of the crime, you only discover these later and make the deduction. The story is nearly over and many of the probable suspects are either dead or behind bars falsely accused -- and then only because the author is diabolically clever enough to string the clues out almost to the end.

A great detective story -- not just a good one -- begins this way and ends with you the reader making the deduction and experiencing the adrenalin rush of excitement doing so -- just before the author tells you.[4]

Piecing together the probable true origin of chess out of the bits and pieces of evidence dismissed or overlooked before has all the makings of one of the greatest detective stories ever written. Banaschak, Cezaux and other chess historians have had the list of most likely suspects for nearly 20 years (hypotheses 1 through 5), which B. summarizes in his 1997 paper. But true to form, a candidate for being the plus one suspect -- the probable true origin of chess -- is just making its appearance, some twenty years late.

Hypothesis 6: The inventive momentum for chess originated in Africa perhaps 72,000 year ago on repeated cycles of inventive evolutionary drift and mutations in its rules and the imagery of its pieces. Descent into its modern form coincides

---

4   Read Sir Arthur Conan Doyle *Sign of the Four* for a classic example of this greatness.

with the continuous migration of Mitochondrial Eve and Y-Chromosomal Adam's near and distant cousins out of Africa and the criss-crossing paths of their descendant's return back flow out of China thru India to the Middle East and Africa. The diffusion window: Trade routes for the movement of weapons, supplies and chess boards running parallel to and, in some cases, overlaying the migratory paths of homo sapiens leaving Africa tens of thousands of years before. Innovative changes to chess piece imagery and rules were randomly transmitted back and forth along these paths.

Why so late with this simple hypothesis? For one thing, not only is real objective history diabolically clever, it's that, and we call her Divine Providence. Objective history also has no reason to be in a hurry to disclose evidence or suspects. Unsettling as the truth may be, historical facts simply do not care if we ever make the correct deduction. From this perspective, Hypothesis 6 is not late. In fact, it could be just on time or maybe even a little early. Secondarily though, the hypothesis is one of several seismic aftershocks from the genomic out-of-Africa revolution in theory now sweeping the scientific community in all fields in all directions.[5] Hypothesis 6 could not come any sooner than now (2015 AD).

Consider then these bits and pieces of fresh evidence:

1. Men and women belonging to five mitochondrial DNA haploid groups left Southeast Africa beginning 140,000 +/-

---

5 https://en.wikipedia.org/wiki/Recent_African_origin_of_modern_humans; https://en.wikipedia.org/wiki/Mitochondrial_Eve

50,000 years ago. Three populated the rest of Africa (L1,L2, L3), including the Nile Valley region of Egypt 60,000 to 90,000 years ago (L3). Two haploid groups (M and N) began migrating out of Africa between 60,000 and 70,000 years ago, populating the Middle East 70,000 years ago and fanning out into India, China and Europe 45,000 to 60,000 years ago.

2. Populating China between 25,000 and 45,000 years ago, descendants of this initial migration began to back flow into the Middle East and Africa 15,000 to 25,000 years ago, settling in trade colonies along a path paralleling the outmigration of their ancestors. Some in this back flow generation reached the Middle East but never turned left to return to Egypt and Africa, traveling on instead further West into Europe 15,000 years ago.

Make the deductions:

3. Invented by one of the L-haploid groups, mancala, a game of skill, and African throw-sticks, a game of chance -- both used for divinations and mental exercise -- began spreading thru out Africa more or less 72,000 years ago[6]. The two games reached Egypt about 46,000 years ago and were combined by members of haploid group L3 into an invention called Senet, a board game for divination using throw-sticks.

---

6 See *Appendix A. A Nash Equilibrium Model of Inventive Evolutionary Drift*

4. Senet, mancala and throw-sticks left Africa traveling together East with haploid groups M and N for divinations and mental exercise, perhaps reaching the Middle East 23,000 years ago and China 13,000 years ago. How do we know the games ever left Africa? We don't, but it seems highly improbable that these courageous and very bright men and women would have left games of divination and mental exercise behind, traveling into the darkness of the unknown with nothing.

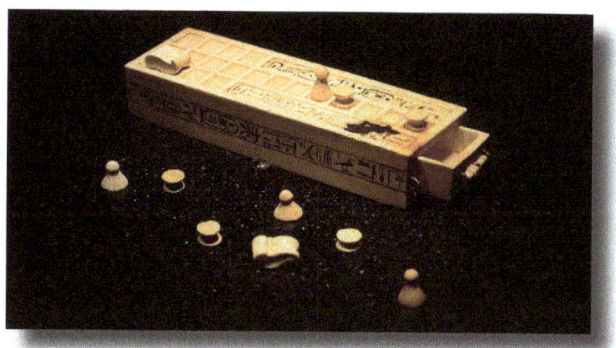

Senet game from the tomb of Tutakhamun 1341 BC-1323 BC

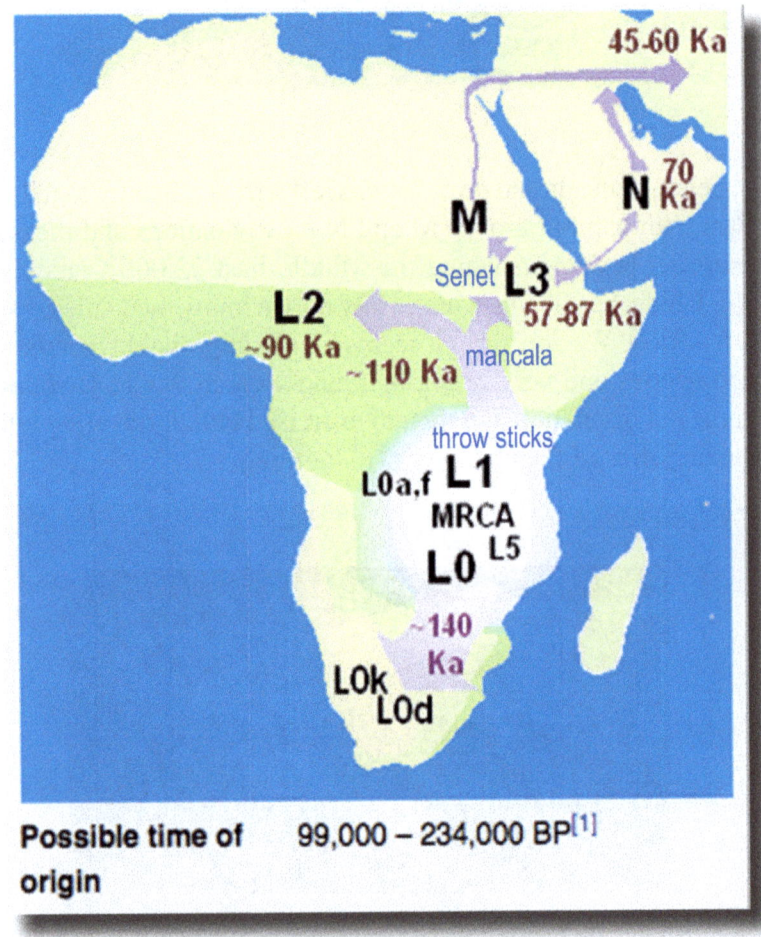

Possible time of origin   99,000 – 234,000 BP[1]

5. In China at least 13,000 years ago, thru a series of inventions over several thousand years, African throw-sticks mutated into I-Ching a method of divination based on chance. Senet mutated into Liubo, perhaps the first and only board game of chance for divination using the sun, moon, planets and stars for its chess piece imagery.

6. During the migratory back flow into the Middle East, Egypt and Africa Liubo, the only astronomy board game of chance for divination we know of, first mutated into Xiangqi chess, a board game of skill for strategic military thinking using elephants, soldiers, generals for chess pieces and then into Xiangxi, its variant. These mutations all ran their course between 2700 BC and 1200 BC. By then Xiangxi chess had become quite popular in India, the Middle East and Egypt. Thanks to this and a series of further inventions, by 500 AD Xiangxi chess had mutated into Persian chess, another board game of skill stripped of divinations for strategic military thinking, its sacred African roots buried and forgotten.

7. By the 12th century AD Persian chess reached Europe and with further minor inventions in chess piece imagery mutated into the chess game we now play using Kings, Queens, Bishops, Knights, Rooks and Pawns. Stripped of both its divinations and strategic military thinking, modern chess is now a simple-minded board game of skill for competition, mental exercise and money. But not without a price: The statistically significant higher than average frequency of Asperger Syndrome among modern chess geniuses.[7]

---

7   G. Moore, *The Gods Play Chess, Don't They?* Chapter I "The Asperger Syndrome"

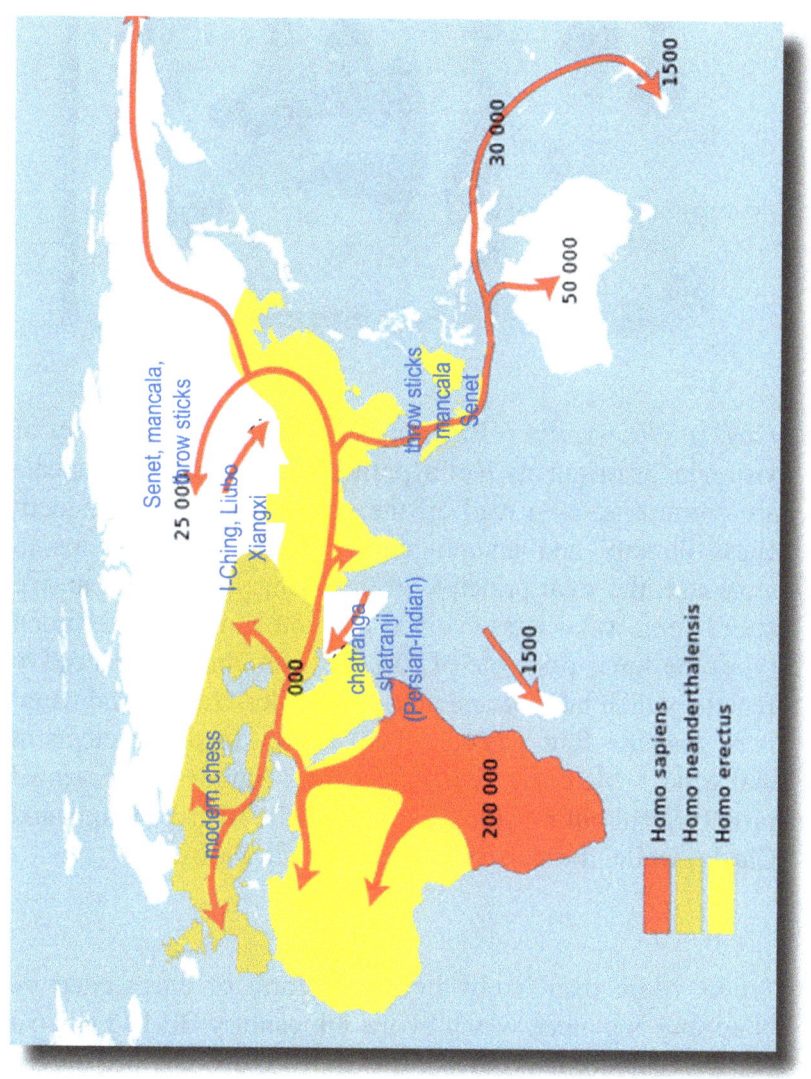

Senet, mancala, throw sticks
25 000

I-Ching, Liubo Xiangqi

chatranga shatranji (Persian-Indian)

modern chess

000

throw sticks mancala Senet

30 000

1500

50 000

200 000

1500

Homo sapiens
Homo neanderthalensis
Homo erectus

Further Observations. First, consider the stunning clarity of vision in the origin myth of hypothesis 1. It is as if the Ancients are permitting us to read off the sacred ancestry of modern chess directly and unambiguously. The sun (ri) seems to represent the solar principle of the changeless and expansive male, Yang, what later evolved into the King, and the moon (yue) the lunar principle of Yin, the ever-changing receptive female, which later became our Councillor-Queen. And could it be that the four planets (chen) visible to the Ancients at that time – Mercury, Venus, Mars and Jupiter – represented prototypes of our modern royal pieces (the Bishop, Knight and Castle) while the stars (xing) were cast as pawns?

Liubo. More than likely the sacred form of chess cited by Niachang is a game which by the 8th century BC had taken a recognizable form. By then it was called Liubo and was played continuously in China up until the 12th century AD. According to one commentator, "although the rules are still largely unknown, some characters are surprising and intriguing: the board was heavily marked and 12 points were distributed around the periphery [to represent the 12] star houses [of the Chinese zodiac].

Also, it appears that the central square was commonly called "the water". Each player was moving 6 stones (qi) as basic Pawns which could be promoted to an Owl (xiao) under obscure conditions. In addition, [the game included] 20 "fish" (zinshi qi) which stayed in the water and had to be captured by the players."

Xiangqi. The secularizing of chess for military purposes captures poignantly the descent of chess from its sacred mysterious beginning. The secular form went by several names, beginning with Xiangxi during the Tang Dynasty, and evolving later into

Xiangqi. While all versions were used for military strategic purposes, one can still observe elements of the esoteric. For example, a kind of color symbolism begins to appear – blue for one army, red for the other. By the time of Bei Song Dynasty in 1000 AD Xiangqi had 16 pieces for each army placed on the intersections of a 8 x 9: cases board, then 9 x 10 points. The pieces were :

1 General (*Jiang* for blue, *Shuai* for red) whose capture, and not divination, had become the aim of the game and which moves 1 step, orthogonally only.

2 Advisors or Mandarins (*Shi*), also confined in the palace and which moves 1 step diagonally (prototypes for the Vizer-Queen).

2 Ministers for blue, or 2 Elephants for red (both named *Xiang* but with different ideograms) which move 2 steps diagonally. (prototypes for our bishop)

2 Horses (*Ma*) whose move is similar to that of our Knights

2 Chariots *(Ju)* strictly equivalent again to our Rooks at the corners of the board.

2 Cannons (*Pao)* placed before most of the troops on the third row

5 Soldiers (*Zu* for blue, *Bing* for red) which step 1 case straight ahead as long as they are in their own half of the board, then which can also move 1 case sideways when they have penetrated the opposite camp (equivalent to our pawns).

In at least one instance the two forms – the sacred and the secular—seem to have collided in time and space. In a 6th century document Wang Bao tells us that chess (referring perhaps to Liubo) was designed to "represent phenomena of heaven and earth, the principles of Yin and Yang, the passing of seasons, the eight trigrams, divination, music, filial piety and loyalty, proper rites, the order of government, and orderly conduct." At the same time the same document tells us that military thinking and strategy played a key role in the game (of Xiangqi).

In its original sacred form if the element of warfare existed in chess as it does now, ancient Chinese chess would have been a strange game indeed. Picture a Blue Sun opposing a Red Sun or a Red Moon tracking down blue stars. And what would it mean for the Divine Farmer to use this warfare in heaven and on earth to pursue his Cosmic Aim?

Lao Tzu on Chess In *Hua Hu Ching* Lao Tzu addressed this question. He tells the story of Pan Kou (another name for Shennong?), one of the first Divine Beings who "shaped the Universe into Heaven and Earth and divided himself into many, many life beings."[23] In tracing this story back to the age of the Yellow Emperor (2697 BC), Lao Tzu gives us the earliest recorded reference to chess. (570 BC – 490 BC)

Pan Kou's name literally means "big round drum". In his Song of Pan Kou Lao Tzu praises the first Divine Being:

Old Pan Kou knows nothing about time and Nothing about space either. Self-natured And self-sufficient he needs to ask for Nothing outside of his own being.
Genesis of worlds is a mental
Exercise for him. When he starts to think,
worlds start to move. This world was never made by special design. Nor has any end ever been put to it. Old Pan Kou just swings his ax and chisels
Rhythmically, and from it comes Heaven,
But not as you think of it, and Earth,
But not as you see it.
Everything is the way it naturally is.

Since the young gods who are descendants of Pan Kou follow only impulse, they make moves that disturb the world. The wise and old ones sit still and watch the chess games of the foolish. All the changes in the world are displayed on the chess board. Victory and defeat are decided by the subtle elements behind the moves. It can clearly be seen by the wise. The wise who love life and value words remain quiet and watch.

*If the foolish gods only knew, there is
perfection before any move is made. It is what offers beings
the opportunity of life.
When an artificial move is made,
The subtle root begins to die. When peace
Is disturbed, the vital energy passes.
The kindness of Old Pan Kou is expressed
As harmony of nature. The further downfall
Of his descendants causes the knowledge
Of the treasures that are hidden in nature
To be lost. They look everywhere for it,
making wasteful competitive moves.*

Two chess games, it seems, are being played and described by Lao Tzu -- that of Pan Kou and that of his descendants, those "foolish young gods who follow only impulse and make "wasteful competitive moves". In contrast, Pan Kou's chess moves are supremely economical, involving the rhythmical motion of a divine being back and forth between Yin and Yang, male and female, expansive energy and contracting receptacle, active and passive, creating the Universe. Lao Tzu describes Pan Kou's chess moves metaphorically as the "swinging of an ax", followed by the chiseling of his being into life forms.

What has this to do with chess as we now know it? Everything and nothing. Everything because "The wise and old ones sit still and watch the chess games of the foolish. All the changes in the world are displayed on the chess board." This includes the "wasteful competitive moves" of modern chess. At the same time, the chess game of Pan Kou has nothing to do with modern chess because it is a game for "wise and old gods" only, a game of strategy where "victory and defeat are decided by the subtle elements behind the moves."

An Indo-Persian Origin? A rival theory has it that chess may have been invented in India thousands of years later. The words for chess in Middle Persian and Arabic are chatranga and sha-tranj respectively, both words derived from *chaturanga* in Sanskrit, meaning "army of four divisions". The out-of-Africa hypothesis gives us scale and perspective on this theory.

To begin with, the earliest Persian references to chess are found in a Middle Persian book *Karnamak-i Artaxshir-i Papakan,* written between the 3rd and 7th century AD. This ancient Persian text refers to Shah Ardashir I, who ruled from 224–241 AD, as a master of the game. Chinese Xiangqi chess was already at least 2,700 to 10,000 years old, conservatively estimated.

Both the Persian and Indian versions of chatranga have two armies of 16 pieces each, with the following setup:

· 1 Shah, whose capture is the aim of the game and which moves 1 step in all direction as our King.

· 1 Vizier (*Farzin, Firzan* in Arab), close to the Shah and which moves 1 step diagonally.

·   2 Elephants (*Pil, Fil* in Arab) which moves diagonally 2 steps, leaping over the intermediate case if occupied.

·   2 Horses (*Asp, Faras* in Arab) moving obliquely exactly as our modern Knights.

2 Chariots (*Rukh* in Persian and Arab) which have exactly the orthogonal move of our Rooks.

·   8 Soldiers (*Piyadah, Baidaq* in Arab) which move 1 step straight ahead (never 2) and capture diagonally ahead as our modern Pawn. When reaching the last row, they are promoted to Farzin ahead (never 2) and capture diagonally ahead as our modern Pawn. When reaching the last row, they are promoted to Farzin.

The most compelling arguments for an Indian origin of chess are based on written texts in Sanskrit and Pahlavi dealing with the game of chess. This theory places the birth of *Chatrang* in North India around the 6th century AD and assumes that it was latter transmitted to China (around 800)   along with other Indian cultural elements However, a rival school claiming a Persian origin for *Chatrang,* bases its claim on the fact that some of the older texts are in Pahlavi, and also because the oldest known chessmen were excavated in Central Asia, then a Persian land.

A Planetary Event. Consider this: the game of chess and its chess pieces have always been planetary in form to the extent that more or less the same pieces were being played in more or less the same way in the major centers of civilization at the same time –today Western Civilization, the Moslem World, Buddhist-Hindu Civilization and in ancient times in Ancient China, Ancient Egypt, Sumer, and India. Even at its alleged birth in the 8th century in Persia, modern chess pieces found in Egypt, India and elsewhere were strikingly similar to their alleged Persian parent more or less at the time of discovery.

The implications: Given its planetary nature, where chess originates is less important than what the pieces mean esoterically at the point of origin, and whether this meaning is transmitted without distortion. This raises an interesting point. Was there ever a layer of inner meaning that somehow became buried and lost at the point of origin? Look at the prototypical chess pieces mentioned in the Chinese monk's document, what do we see: pieces representing the sun, moon, planets, stars. Their likely esoteric meaning to the Ancient Chinese has been discussed already. What could safeguard this meaning? In principle, nothing. Or a principle of invariance.

Invariance of Inner Meaning Across Civilizations. The esoteric meaning of Liubo and earlier chess prototypes may have been buried for a time, but could not be lost forever because this meaning is transparent across civilizations and inevitable changes in imagery and function. Lost for a time, ultimately schools of esoteric thought recover the meaning and transmit it to future generations even though the imagery has been "innovated" on and is quite different. For example, the expansive male principle of divinity embodied in the sun and called Yang by the Chinese was represented by Ra in Ancient Egypt, the receptive female principle of Yin in the moon by Isis/Hathor, the Chinese star houses by the Egyptian divinities Horus, Osiris and Isis in he Southern Sky, and by Sekmet, Seth (or the Thigh of Seth) and Isis in her Hippopotamus form in the Northern Sky.

How could these meanings be lost in the first place? By substitution: For example, replace pieces representing the sun, moon, planets, and star houses with pieces representing generals, ministers, elephants and chariots. With this simple innovation the original meaning is buried. Could this really happen? The historical record is clear, it did happen, and more than once. Then how could the original meaning ever be retrieved? By constructing a kind of Rosetta Stone of chess piece imagery. On the premise that the original meaning is invariant and persists across time and change of imagery as well as civilizations, one can in principle recover this meaning. The *Table of Inventive Evolutionary Drift* below represents one such attempt.

Returning to the mancala hypothesis. Remote as its imagery and functions seem from chess in terms of ancestry, is there nonetheless an objective evolutionary connection between these two games of strategy -- mancala and chess? Chess historian Jean_Louis Cazaux offers a fresh approach to this question. Commenting on the possibility that the Indo-Persian Chatrang and the Chinese Xiangqi may have a common ancestry, Cazaux observes: "For differentiating from [Chatranga and Xiangqi] we must look for a seminal game at more or less the same "structural distance" to both successors. To have existed, such a game should contain the different germs which could have evolved up to Chatranga in one hand and up to Xiangqi in the other hand. That necessarily implies a time span of few centuries." Cazaux adds that thus far "no evidence of the existence of such a game has been found."

Far-fetched as it may seem at first, suppose mancala is, in fact, this common ancestor. After all, mancala is one of the oldest and most widespread board games on the planet. Besides being found throughout West Africa, Egypt and Mesopotamia, remnants have been found in Sri Lanke and other parts of Asia. Played with 6 seed pods, one set for each player and each pod seeded up to 4 seeds at a time, mancala would have been old enough and widespread enough to qualify as a common ancestor. And is it simply coincidence that mancala is played with 6 seed pods while the ancient Chinese game of divination Liubo was played with 6 stones?

If hypothesis 6 is true, mancala originated in Southeast Africa and reached Egypt 46,000 to 72,000 years ago. In Egypt stone mancala boards have been found carved into temples roofs at Memphis, Thebes and Luxor.[13] One theory tells us the game evolved from boards and counters used by ancient Egyptians and Sumerians for accounting and stock taking. Evidence for such record keeping boards have been found in both Mesopotamia and Egypt. Perhaps though, invention runs the other way. Mancala already existed, and record keeping simply became one of its applications.

On the temple roof of Seti I a board game resembling mancala was also found. Completed by Ramses II for his father, Seti I (circa 1320 BC), the temple has numerous game boards hollowed out in sandstone blocks on its roof. Since temple roofs were often used by priests to observe the stars, it is surmised the games were played by members of the Egyptian priesthood.[8]

---

8   On the same temple roof of Seti I with hollowed out mancala boards there is a board consisting of an 8x8 square configuration. How do we know it was a board for chess and not, say, for checkers? Answer: We don't know.

Thus far the oldest evidence for mancala has been found in an ancient Sumerian house excavated by a National Geographic-sponsored team in present-day Jordan. At the site a limestone slab was uncovered with two parallel rows of circular depressions resembling a mancala playing board. The board has been dated to somewhere between 5,000 and 7,000 BC

The crux of the issue. Is mancala an ancient chess prototype? In mancala each player has 6 hollowed out sowing pods. It is the earliest instance we have of a game of strategy, the object being to sow more seeds into your pods than the other player sows into his or hers.[9]

---

9   Jeff Erickson, *Sowing Games, in Games of No Chance*, Cambridge University Press, 1998 [1]. Also: Larry Russ, *The Com-*

The word *mancala* is an Arabic word derived from "naqala" and literally meaning "to move". The name is generic and covers a family of games in Africa and the Middle East. All versions of mancala share in common the strategic principle of counting and then capturing: First count the disposition of your pieces and your adversary's, then seed from your pods to your adversary's, changing the state of the board game to your advantage, and finally capture the most pieces (seeds) based on this changing state.

---

plete Mancala Games Book, Marlowe and Company, NY, 2000 and Philip Townsend, "African Mankala in Anthropological Perspective", *Current Anthropology*, Vol. 20, No. 4. (December 1979), pp. 794-796

Like chess, there are no chance factors in mancala. Player strategy is based on the ability to count and remember the count. Winning involves capturing the most game counters. Strategically, the question is: In how many ways can one seed counters from 6 pods 4 at a time into one or several of the 6 pods belonging to the opponent.

Seeds and seed pods: their esoteric meaning. On one level it makes perfectly good sense for African agricultural societies to invent a board game using seeds and seed pods. What better way to train the next generation? Probing deeper, however, one discovers a hidden meaning as well. The most systematic presentation at this deeper level is to be found among the Dogon tribes of West Africa. There one learns that the Dogon word for "seed" *po* has the same root as the word for "beginning" *polo*.[20] This pun is probably not accidental.

*A statue of King Shyaam Albul Allgoong, founder of
the Kuba kingdom in Central Africa, playing mancala*[10]

The seeds and seed pods of mancala are closely connected
with Dogon creation myths. According to one myth, after the
Supreme Being Amma broke the primordial egg and came
out, He immediately created an oval po seed and located His
Divine Will therein. The seed began spinning, and as it spun,
seeds were scattered in all directions, each containing a germ
of Amma's creative will, each representing in itself a beginning.

10   King Shyaam is said to have taught mancala to his subjects to encourage foresight and calculation. In Uganda, tradition
demanded that every new king play mancala on his ascension to
the throne. This was reckoned a way to test his memory skills and
subtlety in strategic thinking. (Patty A. Hardy, *Count and Capture:
Mancala Boards of the British Museum*, 1997)

Table of Inventive Evolutionary Drift – Random Changes in Chess Rules and Chess Piece Imagery Over Time

	throw-sticks	mancala	Senet	I-Ching	Liubo	Xiangxi/Xiangqi	chatranga/shatranj	modern chess	inner meaning – invariant across time and civilizations
date range of inventive drift	90,000 BC-60,000 BC	90,000 BC-60,000 BC	70,000BC-45,000BC	25,000-15000 BC	25,000-15000 BC	3600 BC-2700 BC	500 AD – 1100 AD	1100 AD – 1300 AD	significant random events are accelerating
		throw sticks to start game	throw sticks to start game	throw sticks to start game	throw sticks to start game	throw sticks to start game	dice to start game	dice to start game	random events based on probabilities represent fate manifesting itself
	light-colored throw sticks, unknown number, function unknown	24 seeds	5 cones	6 unbroken lines	6 stones	1 general	1 shah	1 king	solar-male yang principle of expansiveness, will, emotional intelligence, activeness, open
	dark-colored throw sticks, unknown number, function unknown	6 pods	5 reels	6 broken lines	6 owls	1 vizer	2 advisors	1 queen	lunar-female yin principle of receptiveness, secretive, instinctive intelligence
					12 star houses	2 ministers	2 elephants	2 bishops	principle of careful deliberation, intellectual-instinctive centers
			house of happiness		20 fish	2 horses	2 horses	2 knights	principle of the unexpected, volatile emotions, sudden change of direction
			house of water		house of water	2 chariots	2 chariots	2 rooks	principle of reliable consistent effort
			house of rebirth			5 soldiers	8 soldiers	8 pawns	principle of self-sacrifice for a higher purpose, mechanical I's for Work I's, source of regeneration, pawn becomes queen
						2 cannons			

Within each po seed the act of creating passes thru four phases – conception (the bummo phase), pure form (the yala phase), concrete form (the tonu phase) and the thing itself (toymu). To complete the creation of all things, Amma passes thru 6 bummo or moments of conception, expressing his creative will at each moment in four phases.[21]

For the Dogon it seems the seeds of mancala could represent particles of the first po seed containing the Divine Will, the 6 seed pods its 6 moments of conception, and the seeding of each pod up to 4 at a time a repetition of the four phases of creation.

Conclusion. On a timescale exceeding by at least two powers of ten in depth and complexity anything advanced so far by Standard Models for board games, Hypothesis 6 proposes this: Like abstract art in motion, simple and completely devoid of imagery, mancala with its 24 smooth-surfaced seeds, representing the generative principles of our Universe, and its 6 seed pods, representing the six moments of the Universe's conception, evolved into a Senet game using throw-sticks for dice and game pieces. This happened at some point in time at least 46,000 years ago during the out-of-Africa migrations. While both the meaning of the game pieces (cones and reels) and the rules for playing Senet have been lost, more than likely the pieces were of cosmological significance and the rules allowed players to simulate the motion of the sun, moon and stars for divination purposes. According to this hypothesis, Senet, in turn, mutated into Liubo with its military chess game imagery 12,900 years ago. And a prototype for dice-throwing, African throw-sticks, in turn, mutated into I-Ching about the same time (and then much later into modern dice itself). None of these games were games in the modern sense, they were more like software widgets -- for mental exercise and divinations.

Between 2700 and 1200 BC Liubo began evolving further into Xiangqi on the one hand and Chatranga on the other, losing its connection to the sacred art of divination and be-coming a game of skill for strategic military thinking. The structural distance between Senet and Liubo -- roughly 34,000 years +/- -- was enough to allow time and cultural space for innovations to add 12 star houses, 20 fish, and thecentral waters to the original 5 cones and 5 reels of Senet with its three houses of central waters, happiness and rebirth.

Over the next 10,200 years +/- (between 12,900 BC and 2,700 BC) inventiveness would further differentiate Liubo into the Blue General /White Shah, Vizer, chariots, elephants etc of Xiangqi/Chatranga.

Modern chess would appear in Europe roughly 3,200 years later.[24]

Appendix E. A Nash Equilibrium Model of Inventive Evolutionary Drift

There seems to be a general consensus on the time clock of migrations out of Africa, but neither consensus nor even a discussion of when the three inventions -- throw sticks, mancala and Senet -- first made their appearance. When were these games invented and when did our early ancestors take them to India, Southeast Asia and China? Also, when did this mysterious process of inventive drift and mutation into Liubo and Xiangxi start happening? Can we estimate any of this, knowing more or less when the out-of-Africa migrations happened? Think about it: On the scale of 140,000 years ago, that would leave a lot of room for trial, error and invention -- including errors in our own calculations. There is no question about our African ancestors being mentally equipped to invent these games because the simple fact of the matter is they did. Question is, when?

Fortunately, we have several fragmentary leads, like bits and pieces of the mitocondrial DNA they are based on: 1) The time haploid groups L1 and L2 began migrating out of Southeast Africa and populating North and West Africa (140,000 years ago), 2) the time men and women belonging to haploid group L3 reached the Nile Valley (70,000 years ago) 3) the time Haploid groups M and N began fanning out of Egypt and across the Sina Peninsula 45,000-60,000 years ago and 4) the time descendants of those groups reached China 25,000 years ago, and began backflowing into the Middle East and Africa.

The above consensus represents, in effect, a time clock for estimating the invention and movement of our chess piece ancestors. How can we use it? One strategy is to simply use the clock as is, noting that it gives high maximum estimates. A second strategy, which is adopted in this paper, is to adjust downward these maximum estimates to get closer to the truth, remembering Lewis Carroll's observation, "When you don't know where you are going almost any road you take will get you there" For logical coherence and consistency a Nash equilibrium model of inventive drift has been constructed and used to make the adjustment.

The theoretical model. Does the model work? Let's see:

1) It begins in a state of Nash equilibrium for inventions 140,000 years ago +/-: Imagine a colony in Sutheast Africa with several inventors in it. Not everyone in the colony is an inventor. Just these men (and women). Constantly in communication, they share their strange vision of things with each other all the time. What this or that really is, how to make it work better, why any of it works at all, etc. Prototypical science-engineer-mystics. They see and invent strange things for the colony all the time. Little trivial things, a few significant things. Like a water-resistant dye for cave drawings or flint for making fires or a water-wheel.

Sometimes there is no incentive in any one inventor to invent anything because none sees any benefit in it for the colony over what has been invented already or over what others are thinking about inventing. The incentive to invent = 0, the incentive not to invent = 1, the incentive to invent index = sum(incentives to invent)/sum(incentives not to invent)+1 = 1. The inventors are in a state of Nash equilibrium.

2) Whenever any one or more inventors sees some benefit in an invention for the colony, the state of Nash equilibrium is broken, and there is an incentive to invent. The incentive to invent = 1, the incentive not to invent = 0, the incentive to invent coefficient = sum(incentives to invent)/sum(incentives not to invent)+1 > 1.

3) In a state of broken Nash equilibrium for invention, collectively or independently and alone, inventors would be at work making something work better or differently for the colony. Unlike Athena out of the head of Zeus, however, inventions do not spring ready-made and functioning out of the heads of their inventors. Time would nearly always be a limiting factor. It might have taken months, years, even several generations before the tiny spark of an original incentive became a finished, practical, and more or less zero-defect working invention for the colony. Let's call this the drawing board to functioning product time delay factor, or simply the time delay factor where time delay = no. inventions/[no. incentives to invent + no. inventions]

4) So to adjust downward the haploid group migration estimates from time of migration $T(m)$ to time of invention $T(I)$ simply multiply the haploid migration time $T(m)$ by the incentive to invent index (I) and the invention's time delay factor d. Or simply, $T(I) = T(m) \times I \times d$

$$= T(m) \times \text{Sum(incentives to invent)}/$$
$$\text{Sum(incentives not to invent)}+1 \times \text{no. inventions}/$$
$$[\text{no. incentives to invent} + \text{no. inventions}]$$

A measurement model. Assuming humanity's behavior today is not significantly different from what it was 140,000 years ago, it is safe to further assume that the incentive to invent and the time delay factor limiting it are more or less the same also. Or stated differently, even if there is a difference, this would not alter our conclusions significantly. Accepting this, look at Table 1. It shows the number of patents awarded to independent inventors in the U.S. between 2004 and 2014. 164,942.[1] How many of these patents resulted in finished working inventions? Based on statutory registrations, about 190.

Table 1. Calculating the Nash Equilibrium Time Adjustment Coefficient:
*Nash equilibrium time adjustment coefficient: d = no. inventions/[no. patents + no. inventions]

year	patents to independent inventors	Registered new inventions		
2004	15173	20		
2005	12781	23		
2006	15247	32		
2007	13773	29		
2008	13062	20		
2009	12696	8		
2010	16049	17		
2011	14869	15		
2012	16115	8		
2013	17353	14		
2014	17824	6	time adjustment coefficient d*	
2004-2014 total count	164942	190	0.001151	

Using these counts as proxies, the time delay factor is simply

$$d = 190/(164{,}942 + 190) = 0.001151$$

To understand what this factor means practically for our study, calculate a time of invention for mancala without taking into account the incentive to invent, i.e., let I = 1. Doing this, we discover that the game of mancala would have been invented 161 years ago (Table 2) since $T(I) = T(m) \times I \times d = 140{,}000 \times 1 \times 0.00151 = 161.14$ years ago.

---

1 Source: U.S. Patent and Trademark Office http://www.uspto.gov/web/offices/ac/ido/oeip/taf/data/.

Table 2. Nash Equilibrium time adjustment A: T(n) = T(i) x 1 x d
where d = no. inventions/[no. Patents + no. inventions]
I = Nash incentive to invent = 1

invention	T(i) (years ago)	d	T(n) (years ago)
mancala, throw sticks	140000	0.001151	161.14
Senet	90000	0.001151	103.59
	60000	0.001151	69.06
	70000	0.001151	80.57
	45000	0.001151	51.8
Liubo, Xiangxi	25000	0.001151	28.78

Table 3. Nash Equilibrium time adjustment B. T(n) = T(i) x 100 x d
where d = mo. inventions/[no. Patents + no. inventions]
I = Nash incentive to invent = 100

invention	T(i) (years ago)	100 x d	T(n) (years ago)
mancala, throw sticks	140000	0.115100	16114
Senet	90000	0.115100	10359
	60000	0.115100	6906
	70000	0.115100	8057
	45000	0.115100	5179.5
Liubo, Xiangxi	25000	0.115100	2877.5

A most improbable event. Stated differently, it would have required humanity nearly all of human history, recorded and unrecorded, to invent mancala. Since we know objectively that didn't happen, this confirms indirectly the pivotal game-changing role of the Nash incentive to invent. No pun intended. How big of an incentive to break the states of Nash equilibrium for inventing mancala and the other games? We don't know.

Tables 3 thru 5 give us some indication. They are simulations of possible time paths for inventive evolutionary drift from mancala thru Senet to Xiangxi and chatangra, based on breaking Nash equilibrium at index levels 100 thru 300.

Table 4. Nash Equilibrium time adjustment C : T(n) = T(i) x 200 x d
where d = mo. inventions/[no. Patents + no. inventions]
I = Nash incentive to invent = 200

invention	T(i) (years ago)	200 x d	T(n) (years ago)
mancala, throw sticks	140000	0.230200	32228
Senet	90000	0.230200	20718
	60000	0.230200	13812
	70000	0.230200	16114
	45000	0.230200	10359
Liubo, Xiangxi	25000	0.230200	5755

Table 5. Nash Equilibrium time adjustment D: T(n) = T(i) x 300 x d
where d = mo. inventions/[no. Patents + no. inventions]
I = Nash incentive to invent = 300

invention	T(i) (years ago)	300 x d	T(n) (years ago)
mancala, throw sticks	140000	0.345300	48342
Senet	90000	0.345300	31077
	60000	0.345300	20718
	70000	0.345300	24171
	45000	0.345300	15538.5
Liubo, Xiangxi	25000	0.345300	8632.5

Table 6. Nash Equilibrium time adjustment D: T(n) = T(i) x 447 x d
where d = mo. inventions/[no. Patents + no. inventions]
I = Nash incentive to invent = 447

invention	T(i) (years ago)	447 x d	T(n) (years ago)
mancala, throw sticks	140000	0.514497	72029.58
Senet	90000	0.514497	46304.73
	60000	0.514497	30869.82
	70000	0.514497	36014.79
	45000	0.514497	23152.37
Liubo, Xiangxi	25000	0.514497	12862.43

Is there a maximum Nash incentive to invent? Yes. Letting $T(I)$ = $T(m)$, we discover the maximum incentive is simply

$$I(max) = 1/d = 868.8$$

Using this maximum pushes us to the opposite extreme: The games of throw sticks and mancala would have been invented the very same day men and women of haploid groups L1 and L2 set out for North and West Africa 140,000 years ago.

An equally improbable event.

The final step: Simply sum the incentive to invent indices from the minimum to the maximum and average out the effect of the two improbabilities for inventing mancala -- 161 years ago and 140,000 years ago. We don't know and perhaps can never know precisely where the real historical incentive is, but we do know for certain it is not at the extremes. Table 7 does this. The real Nash incentive to invent may be somewhere around 446.9 +/-94. Table 6 is based on this average, and estimates in the text for times of invention are based on it also.

Table 7. Calculating the Average Incentive to Invent

minimum incentive	1
	100
	200
	300
	400
	500
	600
	700
	800
maximum	868
average	446.9
standard error	94.06

G. Moore
July, 2015
edited: July, 2017

REFERENCES

Nash, John (1950) "Equilibrium points in n-person games" *Proceedings of the National Academy of Sciences 36(1)*

Nash, John (1951) "Non-Cooperative Games" *The Annals of Mathematics 54*

Lightning Source UK Ltd.
Milton Keynes UK
UKHW022010040722
405379UK00010B/194/J